❋ ❋ ❋ THE BIBLE
AND HUMAN SEXUALITY:
CLAIMING GOD'S GOOD GIFT

ELLEN A. BRUBAKER

United
Methodist
Women
FAITH · HOPE · LOVE IN ACTION

The Bible and Human Sexuality: Claiming God's Good Gift
By Ellen A. Brubaker
Participant's Guide by M. Garlinda Burton
© 2016 United Methodist Women. All rights reserved.

For all other requests, contact
Executive Secretary for Spiritual Growth
United Methodist Women
475 Riverside Drive, Room 1501
New York, NY 10115
Phone: (212) 870-3905
Fax: (212) 870-3736

All biblical quotations, unless otherwise noted, are from the New Revised Standard Version (NRSV) of the Bible, copyright © 1989 by the Division of Christian Education of the National Council of the Churches in Christ in the United States of America. Used by permission. All rights reserved.

ISBN: 978-1-940182-38-4
Library of Congress Control Number: 2015953459

Cover design: Rae Grant
Cover image: Evgeny Karandaev

Printed in the United States of America.

United Methodist Women
PURPOSE

The organized unit of United Methodist Women shall be a community of women whose purpose is to know God and to experience freedom as whole persons through Jesus Christ; to develop a creative, supportive fellowship; and to expand concepts of mission through participation in the global ministries of the church.

The Vision

Turning faith, hope and love into action on behalf of women, children and youth around the world.

Living the Vision

We provide opportunities and resources to grow spiritually, become more deeply rooted in Christ and put faith into action.

We are organized for growth, with flexible structures leading to effective witness and action.

We equip women and girls around the world to be leaders in communities, agencies, workplaces, governments and churches.

We work for justice through compassionate service and advocacy to change unfair policies and systems.

We provide educational experiences that lead to personal change in order to transform the world.

✖ Contents

✳ Acknowledgments

Ellen extends heartfelt thanks and gratitude to staff members at United Methodist Women, who have guided her through the process of developing and writing this study. Their guidance, insights, and patience have been a source of support and encouragement. She also thanks her husband, John Ross Thompson, who has contributed his time and expertise in reading and doing preliminary editing as the document was in process. His love and support are a blessing.

✳ Introduction

This study explores the Bible and human sexuality as two essential components of our Christian faith. The Bible is part of the foundation of our faith. Human sexuality is part of who we are as human beings, created by God and called good. Over the centuries, there have been many interpretations of what the Bible says about sexuality and how we should live in our bodies as persons of faith. Some people believe that the Bible is to be understood in a literal way. They believe that God dictated the laws and teachings that tell us what to do if we are to be faithful to God's Word. Others believe that the Scriptures are inspired by God because the spirit of God was at work in the faith of the writers. Inspiration left room for further interpretation by those who have read the Scriptures over the years. The Protestant Reformation was in part about the freedom and responsibility of Christians to read, pray, and seek the meaning of Scripture.

Today we continue to have conflicts in our interpretations of Scripture with regard to human sexuality, so we need to understand where we have come from in order to move into the future. A better understanding of Scripture can help us participate in what our founder, John Wesley, called "social holiness." You can explore this in "Our Theological Task" from *The Book of Discipline of The United Methodist Church 2012*. This is the way we will act out the gospel in our Christian witness.

This study will examine Scripture, beginning with the creation narratives in Genesis 1 and 2. It will proceed through the formation of the law after the Exodus and through the period between the testaments, leading to the coming of Jesus. We will look at what Jesus taught, said, and did. Beyond that, we will study Paul, seeking to understand his writings and his priorities in the development of faith and church. We will also give attention to some of the later writings of the New Testament, which were not written by Paul, and how they support or differ from his views.

We are not finished when we have examined the Bible itself. We must learn how various interpretations of Scripture have affected the church over the years and our current views of faith and sexuality. Doctrines of the early church are a part of the story. What we were taught about sexuality, ourselves, and the church are also a part of the story. What were we taught about the relationship of men and women? Were we taught that in some sense sex is "dirty"? Did we learn to celebrate the harmony of body and spirit, which are both a part of our wholeness in creation?

As this study is being written, we are encountering deep differences in society and within the church over issues related to divorce, gender, abortion, and homosexuality. What are the responsibilities of those who enter into a marriage covenant? What about same-sex couples who love each other, including couples raising families? The Scriptures are a part of our differing interpretations. What do they really say? Looking again into the Bible, the way it was formed, and how it is to be understood in today's world, is a demanding task, but it is one that we need to undertake if we would bear Christ in our own personhood.

Many sisters and brothers who have been at the fringes of the church or outside of it altogether ask this of us. All of us need to read, pray, and live the truth of the Bible as it reflects the love of God in Christ in our time. We need to understand what part of our understanding of sexuality has been defined by culture and what part reflects the vision of God for God's people. Perhaps as we study, pray, and act, we will move toward a sexual ethic defined by a consciousness of Jesus Christ. My prayer is that God will speak to us in our personal lives and in the life of the church as we engage the Bible in this study, and as we witness to a world that is desperate for the good news of the gospel.

❋ ❋ ❋ CHAPTER 1

It Was Very Good: The Creation Stories

Recently, I sat with a beloved granddaughter. She is a young, committed public school teacher with a vibrant Christian faith. She is also in the formation of a love relationship for the first time. I take delight in her joy as she speaks about all these new feelings. When I asked her what she likes best about the special man in her life, she replied that she likes the word "partner," used often by same-sex couples. This young man respects my granddaughter and he is coming to know her as a whole person.

Together, they are striving for mutuality as their love grows. The love of Christ and guidance of the Bible are important to both of them. I also gathered that they will be responsible in determining the role that sexual intimacy will play in their lives. What she has from her parents and grandparents is a trust that faith, grounded in Scripture, will be very much a part of their growing relationship. They understand that, in a genuine, healthy, loving relationship, the lovers are whole persons willing to submit to each other. They see this model of mutuality as grounded in the biblical witness, conveying God's unconditional love for all created life, theirs included.

Now we move backward in time:

Picture a blazing fire lighting the dark of evening in the community. The work of the day is done at last. Little children grow drowsy in their parent's arms. There is an air of expectancy. The storyteller rises from a place near the fire. Tonight's story begins. Once more, the story is told of the God whose love for the world led to the creation of night and day, sun and stars, water and land, plants that provided food, fish in the sea, and animals roaming the land. The storyteller's voice grows more dramatic. Anticipation can be felt around the fire. The storyteller tells how God reflects on all that has been created in intense love and finds something still missing. This great God, who remains mysterious in many ways, desires relationship with the creation. Creation is not finished until it produces life that can respond to the Creator. The voice of the storyteller rises to a crescendo as once again the story is told of the first humans. A man and a woman are blessed and given a beautiful garden to live in and to cultivate in loving and grateful harmony with the God who has breathed into them the gift of life.

We know that centuries of oral tradition, the telling of stories of history and faith, came prior to the written word. This is true of both Israel and its nearby cultures. The stories began long before Israel understood itself as a special "people of God." Biblical scholars are able to determine the various groups of writers who began to produce written accounts of the story traditions by examining the writing styles and theological emphases that reflected their particular communities. Beyond these groups of writers, there were editors who put the stories together in an effort to weave together the various traditions. These were the redactors who added their own interpretations to the material. A vivid example of the way stories came together can be found in the first two chapters of the Bible, Genesis 1 and 2. There are similarities and differences in these two creation accounts. *The New Interpreter's Bible* suggests that Genesis 1:1–24a can be assigned to a writer or writers of the Priestly tradition and Genesis 2:4b–25 to a Yahwistic writer.[1]

In college, I had a professor of religion who had a Bible that was color coded according to what scholars have come to understand as four traditions of writers who were part of the compiling of the Hebrew Scriptures. What scholars noticed was that there were two words for God in the Pentateuch, the first five books of the Old Testament. The first tradition was named the J source after the German spelling for Yahweh (Jahwe), the name used for God. Possible dating for this source was the ninth or tenth century BCE. The E source used

Elohim as the name for God. This source is thought to have originated in the Northern Kingdom in the ninth or eighth century BCE. The P or Priestly source was the third and was likely produced in the exilic or postexilic period. The fourth tradition, the D source, seems to have accompanied a centralizing of the Yahwistic cult and suppression of the Canaanite cults. This occurred over a long time and is also dated in exilic or postexilic times.[2]

THE CREATION ACCOUNTS

There are differences in the progression of creation in the two Genesis accounts. But both creation accounts witness to the relationship between female and male as one characterized by equality and mutuality.

Chapter 1 proceeds in a certain order and culminates in the creation of male and female human beings in the image of God. It is essential to note that being created in the image of God is not becoming God. Rather, it is to be God's representative. *The New Interpreter's Bible* states, "The image functions to mirror God to the world, to be God as God would be to the non-human, to be an extension of God's own dominion."[3]

Genesis 1 reminds us again and again that the creation is good, culminating in the creation of human beings and the admonition to the woman and man to be fruitful and to exercise dominion over all aspects of creation. As the sixth day ends, God pronounces that all that has been made is very good. The language of the naming of responsibility for the humans is one of stewardship and caring for creation, not dominating it for human use alone. Phyllis Trible, biblical scholar and theologian, reminds us that in this section of Scripture the two humans are treated equally. She says, "The context itself identifies two responsibilities for humankind: procreation (1:28a) and dominion over the earth (1:26, 28b), but it does not differentiate between the sexes in assigning this work."[4] In Genesis 1, the man and woman are created at the same time, totally equal and both given responsibility to care for the creation. Thus, "according to our likeness" applies to both.

As we consider the second creation account, we can note that there were similar creation narratives emerging in the writings of other Ancient Near Eastern cultures. A significant difference remains in the unique relationship of God and humanity, however. Other written accounts of the period speak of rulers or other figures in terms of a blending of human and divine qualities. This is not true of the biblical account. Adam is created from the dust (clay) of the earth. Eve is created of the same. The dust of the earth is a living entity, created by God and brought to life on earth.

In Genesis 2, the man (Adam) is created and located in the Garden of Eden where God invites Adam to name all living things. Becoming aware that a partner for the man is missing, God puts Adam into a deep sleep and his partner is created. This is the first instance of sexual differentiation in the account. Genesis 2:18–25 culminates in the man and woman who are now bone of bone and of one flesh. Phyllis Trible says of the passage, "From one comes two; from wholeness comes differentiation. Now, at the conclusion of the episode, this differentiation returns to wholeness; from the two come the one flesh of communion between female and male. Thus Eros is consummated."[5] Both accounts honor the wholeness of human creation, including our sexuality. Sexuality is the human capacity for sexual feelings. Both stories affirm the wholeness of humanity as created by God.

There is no hierarchy mentioned in either chapter. But some interpretive stereotypes of a hierarchy continue in the face of sound biblical scholarship that would remind us of the wondrous act of God that breathed into us the breath of life and created us as sexual beings for relationship with other human beings. As the two live in the garden, they are not ashamed of their nakedness. They have all that they need. They have each other and the abundance of their surroundings. It seems sad that these two beautiful creation accounts are sometimes used to name being female as subordinate to male when their identity as partners is evident in the language of the text. This study will help us to understand that being faithful to the interpretation of Scripture is to perceive the equal worth of all persons, regardless of sex.

Many biblical scholars suggest that the first eleven chapters of Genesis present a theological view of humanity in relationship to God. This seems to be the case in the Garden of Eden with the man and woman who are given the garden and its abundance. The story takes a fascinating turn in Genesis 3 as first the woman and then the man yield to temptation. There are two trees: the tree of life, the fruit of which can cause them to live forever; and the tree that contains the knowledge of good and evil, which is forbidden to humans. We can interpret the desire to know what God knows as "hubris," a pride that mistrusts God's power and God's work. By giving in to temptation, the woman and man become ashamed of their nakedness. They become aware of their limitations. God is revealed as God chooses, not as humanity demands. Here also we get the first indication that enmity will exist between the man and woman and a hierarchy is established (Genesis 3:16–19). Centuries of debate have ensued regarding this passage, much of it reflecting negatively on the woman. She gave in and enticed her husband to sin, say some. At the same time, the passage could reflect the sociology of growing patriarchy in Israel. The "rule" of the man over the woman is part and parcel of the judgment on the man as much as the woman. The biblical writer understood that patriarchy and related ills came as a consequence of sin rather than being the divine intention.[6]

In the twenty-first century, we continue to deal with various interpretations of the garden story. One is the indication for some that the subordination of women was intended as a part of God's punishment for eating of the forbidden tree. Another came centuries later when the sin was deemed sexual in nature. Some have even related sex to what some call "original sin." We will discuss this more fully later as we seek to understand issues around shaming with regard to our behavior as sexual beings.

The first three chapters of Genesis are part of what *The New Interpreter's Bible* calls "The Primeval Story." This suggests universality in the writer's understanding of God's design for creation and the place of humanity in the created world. The stories in these chapters deal with cosmic situations: God-human relationships, human-human relationships, human-nonhuman relationships. The stories relate human response to God, the sin of hubris in human attempts to either reject or ignore the presence of the Creator. There is a common need to receive and respond to the divine presence in the human world.

HUMAN SEXUALITY AND THE DEVELOPMENT OF ISRAEL

I remember a little book in my Sunday school room when I was beginning to learn the stories of the Bible. There was a picture of a man in a long robe, with a beard and holding a wooden staff. They told me his name was Abraham. The man named Abraham was looking into the sky full of stars. I learned that Abraham heard God telling him that he was to take his family, his tents, and his flocks of sheep and goats and leave the place where he lived to go where God led him. In the picture, Abraham seemed to be listening intently.

With Abraham, God seeks to move on from the destruction caused by the flood (see Genesis 9). The rainbow has appeared and God seeks a new beginning with humanity. Abraham is responsive, a covenant is offered, and promises are made. God promises Abraham, "I will make you a great nation, and I will bless you, and make your name great, so that you will be a blessing. I will bless those who bless you, and the one who curses you I will curse; and in you all the families of the earth will be blessed" (Genesis 12:2–3).

Abraham keeps the covenant in listening to and keeping faith with God. Some biblical scholars suggest that the covenant with Abraham is universal in that all the families of the earth are to be blessed through him. At the same time the ongoing story of Abraham and Sarah, Isaac and Rebekah, Jacob, Leah and Rachel, and Joseph in Egypt signifies the beginnings of Israel's story. Thus chapters 12–50 of Genesis move the reader from the "primeval history" to the "patriarchal history" of the biblical story.

In Genesis 12, early in the the covenant between God and Abraham, we read of an incident that is repeated twice in Genesis, by Abraham in Chapter

20 and by Isaac in Chapter 26. Each story involves giving the wife to a foreign leader in order to protect the man of the family. The foreign rulers are portrayed as more just and hospitable than either Abraham or Isaac. Biblical heroes can have feet of clay. Through stories like this, we come to know the attributes and failings of the human family. Where is the voice of Sarah in these incidents? She is silent and acquiesces to her husband's demand. Adultery took place and Sarah was powerless in the situation. The same is true of Rebekah. This truth constitutes a challenge for those who would derive sexual behavior from a literal interpretation of biblical accounts. At God's prompting, Abraham and Isaac are taken to task by the foreign king.

It seems clear that in the development of the covenant of God with humanity, and later with the people considered the chosen ones, the value and worth of women and girls is diminished and the birth of sons is given ultimate importance. As early as Genesis 3, we get the first ranking of the female in the prediction that there will be enmity between man and woman and the woman will suffer pain in childbirth and will be ruled by her husband (3:15–16). Later, we see that the patriarchs could marry several wives as well as adding concubines to their households. At times actual violence and rape happened to women without clear objection that this was not to be tolerated.

In Genesis 19, two angels visit Abraham with a third companion, possibly Yahweh God, and continue on to Sodom, encountering Lot. They intend to spend the night in the square, but Lot invites them into his house. Once in the house, the men of Sodom demand that the men who came to visit be sent out so that the men of Sodom may have sex with them. Instead, Lot offers his two virgin daughters and says the men may do to them as they please. The angels intervene and the men of Sodom are struck blind and cannot find Lot's door to force it open. This passage has been used to condemn homosexuality, but it makes more sense that this is an episode of violence on the part of men who are out of control and ready to rape whomever they can. Lot, who is soon saved with his family, including sons-in-law who are to marry the same daughters he would have thrown to the savage crowd, is never questioned or judged for his willingness to sacrifice his daughters. We come to know through some biblical stories the complexity of the people who act in heroic and far less than heroic ways as the community evolves.

The nomadic existence of the time of the patriarchs continued for many generations. Their stories mark the beginnings of what was to become the nation of Israel and the concept of a chosen people in a special covenant with God. The admonition to be fruitful and multiply was one of necessity to a people who had to struggle with weather, food supply, health issues, and an abundance of enemies. Only the birth of many children could preserve life and a future for the people.

LAW CODES DEVELOP

With the coming of Moses several hundred years later, the Exodus marks the development of a new stage of Israel as chosen people and the codifying of law that would determine the future of the nation. Following the years of desert wandering, the dream of the Promised Land was achieved through war with the Canaanites who lived and worshiped in the same territory. The spiritual warfare was over the Canaanite religious belief and practice. We know now that this was a challenge to Israel over the centuries, often resulting in syncrenistic practice of both faith traditions. This challenge also affected the covenant relationship and the Deuteronomic law that developed over the years.

Old Testament scholar Cheryl B. Anderson discusses the impact of the laws for the Hebrew people as "speech acts of God." [7] Thus, the biblical laws were more than laws that were formed and later written. They were God's word for God's people. They served to form the identity of Israel as a nation. "Biblical laws, therefore, are directive statements that have illocutionary force in the direction of world-to-words. It is that illocutionary force which prompts the hearer to conform his or her actions to the words. In turn, that force, that ability to affect behavior, helps to explain the ability of biblical laws to shape identity."[8] Illocutionary force suggests that these laws are not just good ideas. They are meant to be obeyed and practiced, because they are the words of God to the people.

We look to Leviticus and Deuteronomy to examine the many laws that became binding during the development of Israel as a nation. There are laws that cover every aspect of life. Some are sublime in their hope for a human community that lives as a faithful people of a living God. We still speak of the Jubilee year, when debts are erased and all are free to begin again. There are laws covering hospitality and the treatment of widows, orphans, and those who sojourn in the land. Sabbath practices develop honoring a God who rested after six days of creation and remembering the liberation from Egypt. Some of the laws involved purity, designating what was clean and unclean, particularly having to do with food, as well as purity codes that dealt with the body.

Sexuality as such was affirmed in ancient Israel, especially in the process of procreation. Children were needed to continue and strengthen the community. Barrenness was a great tragedy for women. Sometimes the taint of sin was associated with the failure to bear children. At the same time, purity codes developed, affecting attitudes toward the body, sexual practices of the Hebrew people, and gender issues that ensued from the law codes relating to men, women, singleness, and marriage. Punishment and reward were instituted to enforce such laws. Cheryl Anderson reminds us that, "By punishing some types of conduct and rewarding others, laws shape and define the behavior deemed appropriate for an adherent of that value system."[9]

Bible scholar Michael Coogan says in *God and Sex*, "Within this patriarchal framework, women, daughters, wives, mothers, sisters—were subordinates, and, like younger sons, are often not mentioned. Even when they have narrative significance, they are frequently unnamed: we are never told of Noah's wife, Lot's wife, Jephthah's daughter, Samson's mother, Job's wife, and many other notable women."[10]

Judges 11:34–40 tells the tragic story of Jephthah's daughter. Her father makes a vow and she, nameless, is the one who is sacrificed in order that her father keep the vow.

This occurred during the time of the judges, who were leaders before the monarchy was established. The truth is that the patriarch had that kind of power over his family. As in all patriarchal societies, the family was dependent on the benevolence of the male leader. This was far from true in Judges 19:22–30. A Levite went to claim his concubine who had fled to her father's house. Sometime later they left to return home, and they entered Gibeah but were not welcomed into a home for the night. At last, an old man welcomed them. That night, men of the town come demanding the male visitor for their sexual pleasure. Instead, the old man offers his virgin daughter and the visitor's concubine. The visitor then thrusts his concubine into the crowd where she is gang raped and left for dead at the doorstep. In the morning the master sees her there and says, "Get up, we are going." He puts her on a donkey and proceeds to travel. At some point the woman dies of her injuries. This is an extreme example of the power of a master over a member of the family, but it is in the Scriptures without a word of judgment for the man who surrendered the woman to the brutal violence of the male crowd.

The patriarchal dominance of family life was both economic and spiritual. The family was an economic unit based on a male ownership hierarchy. There may have been good reasons for a structure that was meant to lead to prosperity for all its members. Without leadership, chaos could ensue. At the same time, as has been indicated above, the spiritualizing of the hierarchal laws clearly contributed to the vulnerability of those marginalized in the hierarchy. Why else would a daughter allow herself to be sacrificed because her father made a self-serving vow? While mothers achieved some authority in their families, daughters were economic units for their fathers to use in transactions with potential husbands or even owners if the father chose to sell his daughter into slavery.

Deuteronomy 22:28–29 states, "If a man meets a virgin who is not engaged, and seizes her and lies with her, and they are caught in the act, the man who lay with her shall give fifty shekels of silver to the young woman's father, and she shall become his wife. Because he violated her, he shall not be permitted to divorce her as long as he lives." Upon examination, we might ask questions of the passsage. Why does the father get the money? Does she really want to marry him after she has been violated? Why is she included in being caught in the act if she has had nothing to say about what happened? While this law may seem to offer a sort of protection for women by being wedded for a lifetime, it also, upon closer examination, leaves a woman being forced to marry her rapist. Riane Eisler puts it this way, "If we look at this law objectively, in the social and economic context in which it was enacted, it is evident that it did not stem from any moral or humane considerations. Rather, it was designed to protect men's property rights in 'their' wives and daughters."[11]

Although the biblical incidents of violence toward women in tribal culture may be few, there were clear limitations on women's freedom of choice and on their identity as children of God equal to all God's children. There were laws pertaining to virgin daughters who only fulfilled their destiny by arranged marriages and giving birth to children, particularly sons. Some laws covered the demand of virginity only for the bride (Deuteronomy 22:13–19). If an engaged virgin was forced into sex with a man not her fiance, both were to be stoned, the man for having sex with another man's intended and the woman because she failed to cry out (Deuteronomy 22:23–24).

Many of us have heard of the practice of Levirate marriage (Deuteronomy 25:5–10). A woman who was widowed was often expected to marry a younger brother and to produce children who would honor the brother who had died. This could continue if the second brother were to die.

Divorce was the perogative of the husband only. Deuteronomy 24:1–4 speaks of a woman who does not please her husband being handed a bill of divorce.

The wife was permitted to marry again if she received a bill of divorce from her husband, but she was not allowed to initiate divorce proceedings.

Why should we in the twenty-first century pay so much attention to the law codes of the ancient Hebrews? Literal interpretations of biblical laws are still practiced in many parts of the world. They may still be taught to our children as they mature as sexual persons. Some of the laws reflect solidarity and a sense of justice for the community, while others cause shame or hardship for individuals without voice or power. At the moment, sexuality is the central biblical background, as interpreters everywhere are asked to take sides on a whole host of sexual-political questions:

Should we be for or against gay marriage, for or against the availability of abortion, for or against the submission of women to their husbands, and for or against women's political leadership? Should we build policies assuming that our commitment to premarital virginity and abstinence can be mandated for all, or will sex education and informed consent lead young people to make healthy choices? Should we prevent gays and lesbians from serving as ordained clergy, or can God's call include everyone, irrespective of sexual orientation or gender identity? If women play the submissive role in relationships, what does this mean for men? How do we define sexual freedom or choice, for women, for men? What side is the Bible on? These questions and others arise from our contemporary views of sexuality and the challenges of a changing world with regard to sexual behavior.

Any view of womanhood that denigrates the God-given creation of either sex diminishes the goodness of creation. We will continue to see the ramifications of these views as we consider the time of Jesus' earthly ministry and the development of the church. But first, it is important to pay attention to the stories of some of the women who became biblical heroes, even in a culture characterized by the dominance of men who were the patriarchs.

THE TRAGEDY OF BARRENNESS

Early in the Scriptures we discover the importance of producing legitimate sons within the ethnic group. We first consider women who lived with the failure to bear children; the one expectation of a woman in the culture. Sarai, who becomes Sarah, is the first to be barren into old age. She has given up hope of having a child, a son. She gives her maid, Hagar, to Abraham and Ishmael is born. Sarah may claim him as a son because Hagar belongs to her as a servant.

Ultimately, God promises Abraham that he will be the father of a great nation, indicating that a "true" son will be born to Sarah. The three visitors come to visit, and the one that is possibly Yahweh God tells Abraham that Sarah will conceive. We remember that she laughs as she hears the promise. God asks why she laughs and then tells Abraham, "Is there anything too wonderful for the Lord?" (Genesis 18:14).

There are other biblical stories of women who have nearly given up hope of having a child. Rachel, who must wait fourteen years to marry Jacob, is late in giving birth to Joseph. Leah and the maids, Bilhah and Zilpah, have all had children belonging to Jacob. The Scripture says that God then remembered Rachel and she conceived and gave birth to Joseph, saying, "God has taken away my reproach" (Genesis 30:23b).

In 1 Samuel 1, we hear what is perhaps the most poignant story of barrenness in the Scriptures. Once again we encounter two wives, Peninnah and Hannah, married to Elkanah. Peninnah has children; Hannah does not. Elkanah loves Hannah despite her childless condition. As Hannah prays, the priest Eli hears her and assures her that God will grant her the child she prays to conceive (verse 16). Her petition is granted. Hannah promises to take her son to the shrine at Shiloh as soon as he is weaned, and she fulfills her promise, saying, "For this child I prayed; and the Lord granted me the petition I made to him . . . " (1 Samuel 1:22). "Therefore I have lent him to the Lord; as long as he lives; he is given to the Lord" (1 Samuel 1:27).

There are other instances of the miracle of birth to women thought to have lost God's favor, including the New Testament story of Elizabeth and the birth of John the Baptist when she and Zechariah had given up hope of a family. God's grace was the component that could rescue the woman and restore her to a respected place in the community.

OTHER HEBREW WOMEN OF FAITH

Another story involving marriage and the birth of a child comes in another form as we read of Ruth and her mother-in-law, Naomi. The familiar story begins in a journey into Moab by Elimelech and Naomi because of a famine. Both of their sons marry women of Moab, and both sons and Elimelech die.

Naomi plans to return as a widow to Judah. Daughter-in-law Orpah returns to her mother's house, but Ruth refuses to leave Naomi. Thay make the journey to Judah and Naomi declares to the women that she is now to be called Mara, as the Lord has dealt bitterly with her. A widow had little status in the community, especially without sons to look after her. Subsequently Ruth, gleaning in the field for grain to make bread, meets Boaz. He favors her and comes to know her story. Despite her foreign blood, her loyalty as a daughter-in-law is respected by Boaz.

Subsequently, through creative planning by Naomi, Boaz marries Ruth and Ruth bears a child, Obed. At Obed's birth, the women celebrate with Naomi, saying to her, "Blessed be the Lord, who has not left you this day without next-of-kin; and may his name be renowned in Israel! He shall be to you a restorer of life and a nourisher of your old age; for your daughter-in-law who loves you, is more to you than seven sons, has borne him" (Ruth 4:15). Obed is the father of Jesse, the father of David.

What makes these women memorable is their willingness to risk and their courage in using what is available to them to make a difference for the choosing of life. God has put the choice before the people. "I call heaven and earth to witness against you today that I have set before you life and death, blessings and curses. Choose life so that you and your descendants may live" (Deuteronomy 30:19). Despite negative teachings with regard to sexuality, they use that very gift to affect life and the community of which they are a part. Some of these women never give up their hope of creating new life with God. Other stories of women describe ways of using sexuality to save others. Who can forget the story of Esther who literally, along with her cousin Mordecai, saves her people?

Vashti, the favored wife, also shows a form of courage when she refuses to come at the command of King Ahasuerus. Her disobedience was said to have ramifications far and wide as it would tempt other wives to disobey their husbands. Vashti is deposed as queen, and a search commences for virgins who will be groomed for a year and then be brought before the king so that he can choose a new queen. Of course, being brought before the king meant brought in the evening and dismissed in the morning (Esther 2:13–14). The women involved had little to offer except for their looks. Even so, the king loved Esther and had her crowned queen.

Soon after comes the plot of Haman to destroy the Jews in the provinces ruled by Ahasuerus. Mordecai appeals to Esther because of her position of power with the king. She tells him that one must receive the golden scepter before going before the king. She is reluctant at first, due to the danger to herself. Mordecai sends her a message saying, "If you keep silence at such a time as this, relief and deliverance will rise for the Jews from another quarter, but you and your father's family will perish. Who knows? Perhaps you have come to royal dignity for just such a time as this" (Esther 4:14). How many times since has someone understood that they were the one who had come for such a time? Esther gains entrance to the king and Esther arranges a banquet where Haman and his plot are exposed. The Jews are saved. She used what she had been given, risking all on behalf of her community.

In the second chapter of Joshua, we learn of Rahab. She, however, is a foreigner and a prostitute who also risked her life to save Jewish spies. This is an exciting story of intrigue and courage as Rahab serves the cause of Israel. For helping them escape, she asks for the safety of her family when the army comes. Rahab is honored in Israel for her courage. Her position as a prostitute makes little difference to the story.

There is a pair of women who must be named as a part of Israel's victories in time of war (Judges 4 and 5). Israel had to struggle for decades to secure its place in the Promised Land. There were wars upon wars, before and after Israel became a nation. In the time of the judges, before Israel had a king, the one female judge we know of was Deborah. Her position indicates that some women rose above the restrictions of the law when their leadership was needed on behalf of Israel. Deborah partners with Jael to lead Israel to victory. Judges 5:7b names Deborah a "mother in Israel." We may find it problematic that some of these women in Scripture play a part in military conquest by Israel. Yet they contributed to what they believed to be God's will for Israel and for the people of God who had been promised a land flowing with milk and honey.

Other women were important to the Israelite community. There were the midwives in Exodus, Shiprah and Puah, who let the baby boys live, going against the commands of Pharaoh.

Tamar was to be given to Selah but becomes pregnant by Judah, her father-in-law, who mistakes her for a prostitute. She saves her life and the lives of her twins by confronting Judah with tokens she had gotten from him at the time of intercourse (Genesis 38).

In 1 Kings 22, we encounter Huldah, who shares the prophetic title with two other women, Miriam and Deborah. The "Book of the Law," recovered from the Temple, is brought to Huldah. No one else has been able to read and interpret the words. Huldah interprets the book that speaks of the wrath of God at the lack of faith in Israel. The king tears his garments and the people come to hear the reading of the book, which begins the reforms of Josiah. Huldah was too significant to the history of Israel not to name. She shares her place in the history of Israel with the women mentioned above who were named while so many women were left to us as unnamed wives, sisters, daughters, in-laws, slaves, and virgins. Such stories help us today in telling the stories of both men and women who have been faithful to God in various ways.

The Hebrew Scriptures tell us the stories of women and men, faithful to their understanding of God's presence in their lives and in their communities. How are we to interpret these Scriptures for our sexuality in the twenty-first century? The biblical writings are not always one dimensional or consistent. We then must focus again on the creation story that brought us our humanity and called it good, very good. This includes us as whole persons, body, mind, and spirit. We find this creative understanding of the gift of our sexuality most beautifully expressed in the Song of Songs, a surprising addition to the Hebrew canon.

THE SONG OF SONGS/THE SONG OF SOLOMON

For centuries, scholars and other students of biblical literature have pondered this book of poetry that somehow survived the winnowing process and made it into the canon of the Hebrew Scripture. We cannot consider the Bible's view of sexuality without the Song of Songs. It may puzzle us, bother us, even embarrass us in contemporary times, but it cannot be ignored because it is there. In her commentary on Song of Songs, Renita J. Weems, a Hebrew Bible scholar coming from the African Methodist Episcopal Church, reminds the reader that it is hard to date the poetry contained in the Song of Songs.[12] There are some similarities to ancient Egyptian love poetry dating from 1500 to 1000 years BCE.

Scholars have placed the book within the wisdom tradition in biblical litera- ture. Much of the wisdom tradition asks more questions of the divine-human relationship than it provides answers. We think of Job questioning why the innocent suffer and Ecclesiastes concluding that all is vanity, and there is no answer to our deepest questions. The Song of Songs is said to be an examination of love and our need to be loved, body and soul. This book stands in sharp contrast to many of the purity laws that regarded bodily functions that came from sexual intercourse as unclean under the law. Ritual purification was needed to cleanse the body from sex. For women, the need to be cleansed was also associated with menstruation and childbirth. Contrast this with Song of Songs, which paints beautiful pictures of the body in the process of love and desire. There is an atmosphere in the relationship of the couple that deems the body a sacred part of life. It is essential to incorporate such love poetry into our understanding of the Scriptures as we seek to discover God's design for the gift of sexuality and the gift of our bodies. It is just as important in the present as it was when it was written.

The name of Solomon is used several times in the book. Solomon's reputation was one of wisdom and as a composer of proverbs and other wise sayings. He was also the husband of hundreds of wives and more women who were his concubines. Perhaps the writer or writers of the poetry of Song of Songs is confident that King Solomon had broad acquaintance with affairs of the heart. At any rate the clear protagonists in the book are dark-skinned lovers who long for each other and describe their love in detail. Some scholars suggest that the poetry is similar to the intense poetry in ancient Egyptian collections. Other scholars compare them to Arabic songs called *wasfs* sung at weddings.

What is exceptional about the Song of Songs is that the female lover has the greatest number of lines in the poetry. She begins, "Let him kiss me with the kisses of his mouth. For your love is better than wine" (1:2). Renita Weems suggests in her reflection on this verse that, "Audiences are invited to identify with a female protagonist who longs to be kissed and swept away by her lover."[13] Her lover, a shepherd, answers back as he describes her beauty in glowing terms, "I compare you, my love to a mare among Pharaoh's chariots. Your cheeks are comely with ornaments, your neck with strings of jewels" (1:9–10).

Each lover continues to describe the other, speaking of the body as a beautiful gift of one to the other. He speaks of her mouth, her neck, her lips, and her breasts that are "like two fawns, twins of a gazelle" (4:5). She, in turn, speaks of his body in the same passionate terms. "His head is finest gold; his locks are wavy, black as a raven. His eyes are like doves beside springs of water, bathed in milk, fitly set. His cheeks are like beds of spices, yielding fragrance. His lips are lilies distilling liquid myrrh. His arms are rounded gold, set with jewels. His body is ivory work, encrusted with sapphires. His legs are like alabaster columns, set on bases of gold" (5:11–16).

The lovers speak of their longing to be together. The poetry is both intimate and erotic. This poetry is full of passion with no shame for the love being expressed. A familiar passage expresses the desire for the lovers to be together:

> My beloved speaks and says to me, 'Arise, my love, my fair one, and come away;
> For now the winter is past, the rain is over and gone.
> The flowers appear on the earth; their time of singing has come, and the voice of the turtledove is heard in our land.
> The fig tree puts forth its figs, and the vines are in blossom; they give fragrance.
> Arise, my love my fair one, and come away.' (2:10–13)

The poetry also suggests that the love of these two is not without challenges. There may be those who do not approve of their love. The reasons are not explained. We only hear the desperation of the lovers to be together despite any threat to their relationship. The woman is the most persistent in calling him to come to her. She is a strong, confident woman who knows who she is and what she desires. This unnamed woman is an example of strength, unusual in biblical literature. She is willing to risk all the challenges to the love relationship with her shepherd. Above all else, Song of Songs argues for love that endures all the impediments and frustrations that may exist in the face of love at its deepest levels.

The conclusion of the book expresses love that has more power than death, leading some scholars to speculate that the poetry might have its origin in a ritual or fertility rite to ward off death.[14]

> Set me as a seal upon your heart, as a seal upon your arm;
> for love is as strong as death, passion fierce as the grave.
> Its flashes are flashes of fire, a raging flame!
> Many waters cannot quench love, neither can floods drown it.
> If offered for love all the wealth of one's house, it would be utterly scorned. (8:6–7)

Song of Songs celebrates love relationships in the human community. There is no indication that the lovers are married; it is more likely that they are not, based on the distance expressed and the desire of the woman for him to come to her. Renita Weems comments that, "The poet is apparently sympathetic to the lovers' desire to plead for their right to love whom they choose, irrespective of norms and prejudices, and to their desire to explore their love. But the composer also respects the power that the combined weight of custom, tradition, and attitudes has to distort even the most laudable attempts at reform."[15]

This book of poetry has puzzled and alarmed people of faith through the centuries. There have been many attempts to suggest that Song of Songs can't possibly mean what it says. After all, did not Adam and Eve become ashamed of their nakedness? Many people have been taught that such erotic expression is not biblical. Some in Israel came to interpret the poetry as an allegory for God's relationship with Israel. In early Christianity there were those who believed the book to be an allegory of the relationship between Christ and the church.

What is there for us to discern if we let Song of Songs speak for itself? The poetry teaches us that our bodies are good, a part of human loving. It teaches us of the power of the passion that is a part of the human experience. It teaches us that even when challenges arise from culture or tradition, love that is deep and true continues to be a reality. Surely the words and images of Song of Songs have something to say to us of God's creation of human life and love that God called very good. It is important for us to see in Song of Songs how some Scriptures flow from the concept of God's love, goodness, and grace, just as it is important for us to recognize when other Scripture passages (or particular interpretations of passages) are not helpful to individuals or to the community as each seeks to grow in Christ.

We move on then to the Christian tradition, discussing the coming of Jesus the Christ and the witness through his life and teachings.

Endnotes

1. *The New Interpreter's Bible* (Nashville: Abingdon Press, 1996), 1:340.
2. Bruce M. Metzger and Michael D. Coogan, *The Oxford Guide to the Bible,* entry D, (Oxford: Oxford University Press, 2002), 147.
3. *The New Interpreter's Bible*, 1:345.
4. Phyllis Trible, *God and the Rhetoric of Sexuality* (Philadelphia: Fortress Press, 1978), 19.
5. Ibid.,104.
6. *The New Interpreter's Bible,* Terence Fretheim, 1:354-364.
7. Cheryl B. Anderson, *Women, Ideology and Violence* (New York: T & T Clark International, 2004), 5.
8. Ibid., 6.
9. Ibid., 13.
10. Michael Coogan, *God and Sex: What the Bible Really Says* (New York: Twelve Hachette Book Group: 2011), 23.
11. Riane Eisler, *The Chalice and the Blade* (San Francisco: Harper, 1987), 96.
12. Renita J. Weems, "The Songs of Songs: Introduction, Commentary and Reflections," in *The New Interpreter's Bible*, 5:361–434.
13. Ibid., 5:380.
14. Bruce M. Metzger and Michael D. Coogan, *The Oxford Guide to the Bible,* 709.
15. Renita J. Weems, "The Songs of Songs: Introduction, Commentary and Reflections," *The New Interpreter's Bible*, 5:434.

⁂ ⁂ ⁂ Chapter 2

The Human Face of God: Jesus the Christ

BETWEEN THE TESTAMENTS

The centuries following the return of the Hebrew people from Babylon brought changes to the patterns of life among the Jewish people. There were major efforts to assure the purity of the Jewish community. In Ezra 9 and 10, we read of the abomination of intermarriage among the various "peoples of the land." "For they have taken some of their daughters as wives for themselves and for their sons. Thus the holy seed has mixed itself with the peoples of the lands, and in this faithlessness the officials and leaders have led the way" (Ezra 9:2).

In Ezra 10, the heads of families meet and in an orderly fashion send away all foreign wives and their children. The men sacrifice a ram as a guilt offering for the sin of mixing foreign blood with that of the chosen people. There is no information as to what may have happened to the women and children sent away.

In the New Testament, we learn of the antagonism toward "peoples of the land," finding expression later in the hatred between Jews and Samaritans. The Samaritan faith grew among the Jews who remained after the Assyrians conquered the Northern Tribes and scattered the population. Some stayed in the area while people of other cultures and nations were sent into the land. The resulting community practiced a faith that was considered a syncretism that diluted the pure Judaism of Israel. The Samaritans interpreted Torah for themselves and built a temple of their own on Mount Gerizim. They did not acknowledge the authority of the scribes, Pharisees, and Sadducees we meet in the stories of Jesus' earthly ministry.

During these years, Greek and later Roman armies reached into the lands of the Jewish faithful. Philip and Alexander, of Macedonia, were military leaders who were dominant for a time. Young Alexander dreamed of conquering the entire world and did in fact conquer a wide swath of the Ancient Near East. Following Alexander's death, a family named Ptolemy ruled Egypt. For a time, Palestine was ruled from the throne of Egypt.

Another successor to Alexander the Great, later to determine events in Palestine, was one of his generals, Seleucus, who was given a territory that "stretched from northern Syria to the borders of Egypt."[1] In 167 BCE, the Seleucid ruler, Antiochus IV Epiphanes, sought to exterminate the core of the Jewish faith. This oppression of the faith led to the resistance of the Hasmoneans, a term applied to a family called the Maccabees.[2] The Hasmoneans took the Temple back in 164 BCE and ruled until 63 BCE, reestablishing Judea as an independent state for a time. Hasmonean rule came to an end when the Roman general, Pompey, conquered Jerusalem.

By the time of Jesus' birth, the Herod family, who were puppets of Rome, was ruling in Galilee and Jerusalem. There was Jewish heritage in the Herod family, but more significant was their loyalty to Rome.

Jesus was born into a time of unrest and turmoil in Palestine. The laws regarding purity continued to be followed. Women were still considered subordinate to men, with a few heroic female exceptions. In Matthew's genealogy, women are mentioned along with men. These will be discussed later. Other women such as Sarah, Rachael, Rebekah, and Esther are honored in the tradition. In the synagogues of Jesus' time, women who attended worship did so in the balcony along with children. Archeologists have discovered many such synagogues in their explorations. The tradition of the separation of men and women continues today in ultra-orthodox Jewish worship.

The tradition assigned separate roles for women and men with only men coming into adulthood through the bar mitzvah. The tradition does not seem to have considered that women, as well as men, have the need to worship God and know the Scriptures. However, women lead in the prayers at home. The bat mitzvah for girls was developed in the nineteenth century and is now celebrated in most Reform and Conservative synagogues.[3]

THE BIRTH NARRATIVES

The Incarnation is God's gift of the Son entering into human history that we might know God more fully in human experience. Each of the four Gospels tells the story with a particular point of view. Only Matthew and Luke refer to Jesus' birth and to his mother's virginity. Discussion of the virgin birth is absent from the other two Gospels and is not mentioned by Paul or the later epistles.

Matthew relates the coming of Christ to the prophecies of the Hebrew Scriptures. Jesus is the fulfillment of God's promises to the chosen people, now expanded to include the Gentiles. The gospel begins with a genealogy that traces Jesus back to Abraham through David, culminating in his father, Joseph, the husband of Mary. Jewish people today trace their lineage through the maternal line, but Matthew seems intent on the paternal heritage. It is also interesting that he includes five women in the genealogy. In addition to Mary, they are Tamar, Rahab, Ruth, and Bathsheba.

Tamar was the woman who tricked Judah, her father-in-law, into fathering her son, Perez, who was later incorporated into the messianic line (Genesis 38). Rahab was a Gentile and a prostitute who saved the Jewish spies (Joshua 2). Ruth was from Moab and became the mother of Obed, grandfather of David. Bathsheba was the wife of Uriah the Hittite (2 Samuel 11). We cannot know for sure Matthew's purpose in including the five women in the genealogy, but it is suggested that he may have wanted to remind readers of the inclusion of Gentiles in the Jewish heritage.

Sexual irregularity was also a part of the birth stories through the women included in the line. Tamar played a prostitute in order to get Judah to do the right thing. He called her righteous when he discovered the truth. Rahab was a prostitute. Ruth was a Gentile from Moab and with Naomi's help seduced Boaz. Bathsheba, seduced by David, was married to a Hittite. Her marriage to a Hittite would have condemned her in some Jewish interpretation, along with her adultery. Yet she became the mother of Solomon. *The People's New Testament Commentary* suggests that Matthew might have included these situations of sexual irregularity to defend the special circumstances of Mary's pregnancy by the Holy Spirit.[4]

There are other issues to be cited in the birth story in Matthew. The engagement of Mary and Joseph was already a legally binding agreement in first-century Judaism. "Betrothal was treated as a binding arrangement and reputations could suffer if the reason for dissolving it involved moral shortcomings" (Matthew 1:18–19).[5] When Joseph learns of Mary's pregnancy, he decides to put her aside quietly. The harsh sentences in the law codes could be softened in those days, but not always, as we discover later when Jesus is confronted with the woman caught in adultery. In a dream, Joseph is enlightened as to the true nature of Mary's condition, and he takes her as his wife.

It is important to ask why a virgin birth is essential for Matthew and later Luke. The word "*bethulah*" in Hebrew means either "virgin" or "young girl or woman." Usually the Hebrew Scriptures make clear the virginal state by adding phrases such as "had never slept with a man" (Genesis 24:16, Judges 11:39, 21:12).[6] In cultures in and around Palestine, there were frequent references to miraculous births. There were male gods who impregnated mortal females, giving birth to heroes such as Hercules, Augustus, and other figures, both mythical and real. There may have been an intention to highlight the birth of Jesus, Son of God, in a notable way. "Also the numerous reports of virginal conceptions of mythological figures, such as Heracles or Perseus, or of such historical figures as Alexander the Great, Apollonius, or even Plato could have motivated Jesus' followers to have him recognized as the offspring of a god."[7]

However, the birth narratives are not stories of a male god impregnating a human female. Mary becomes pregnant by the power of God through the Holy Spirit. Matthew emphasizes the fulfillment of prophecy in this sacred event, "Look, the virgin shall conceive and bear a son, and they shall name him Emmanuel" (Matthew 1:23).[8] This is consistent with Matthew's desire to link prophecy in the Hebrew Scriptures with the coming of Jesus; his birth, life, and ministry; death and resurrection. The linkage of earlier prophecy with New Testament theology is always a topic for interpretation and discussion. It is important to know what the prophecy meant in the time that it was written, just as knowing the context may be significant for future events.

Another issue to consider in the birth narratives is more closely tied to the perceived negative aspects of human sexuality. Menstruation made a woman unclean. Intercourse made both parties impure. According to the purity codes, the rupture of a woman's hymen brought about bleeding and the end to the virginity of the woman. In Chapter 1, we discussed rituals of cleansing needed after menstruation, intercourse, and childbirth before one could return to the community. There would have been then, as there is now, a sense that God's divine Son would not be born in such an impure human process.

Luke's Gospel deals with Jesus' birth in ways that are different from Matthew's. In the first place, he traces the lineage back to Adam (Luke 3:23–38). No women are mentioned and a parenthetical comment is added, noting that Joseph is the father of Jesus. He takes pains to point out the world setting into which Jesus is born, and places his genealogy immediately after Jesus' baptism. The emphasis in Luke is on Mary's obedience to the will of God.

The well-known Christmas story is told. Again, the rites of purification are followed after the birth of Jesus before he can be brought to the Temple. Luke reminds us of the taint of birth and blood that must be cleansed before life can be resumed (Luke 2:21–24).

What began in the birth narratives of Matthew and Luke compounded itself through the centuries. Jennifer Wright Knust in *Unprotected Texts* discusses the virginity of Mary according to some early Christian writers.

She speaks of the Proto-Gospel of James, indicating that Mary was never tainted by menstruation during her life. According to this book, she was pregnant before menses occurred and was not defiled by delivery of the infant Jesus. On the other hand, Tertullian, a North African theologian working in the second and third centuries, wrote that the "exceptional filth of childbirth, a filth that plagues both Mary and all women, is taken as an exceptionally convincing proof of the mercy of a God who would not shrink even from the dirt of a woman's womb."[9] Either way the natural process of conception and birth is thought to defile women.

The main reason to discuss the birth narratives here is to determine what they mean for us today in this study of sexuality. Many of us have been confused about them quite early in our lives of faith. I know that I learned early on that there were people of faith who believed fully in the literal accounts of Jesus' birth in Matthew and Luke. Others did not. How could one recite the Apostle's Creed if one doubted?

What about Mary? Did she have other children? Protestants believe that Scripture speaks of Jesus' brothers and sisters coming to see him and asking to speak with him. Some believed these to be cousins. This second view supports the belief in Mary's perpetual virginity. Scripture also talks about Mary and Joseph not "coming together" until Jesus was born (Matthew 1:25). What about the relationship of Joseph and Mary? Isn't the birth of a child in the natural way a miracle also? Why would God who chose to be among us in human form choose a different way for Jesus to be born?

Later, I came to learn more about the attitudes toward sex and the negative teachings about some ordinary human bodily functions. If God created the process of the creation of new life, why is it bad? Michael Coogan says, "This emphasis on Mary's perpetual virginity further illustrates the negative attitude toward sex that has characterized much of Christian teaching for two millennia."[10] Coogan also suggests that the later elevation of Mary by church leaders may have had to do with the need to highlight the feminine aspects of God, to complement the prevailing emphasis in biblical interpretation on male characteristics of God. (The personification of Wisdom as a female characteristic of God in wisdom literature is an important exception to the rule.)

In some Christian traditions, Mary, a virgin, becomes pregnant by the power of the Holy Spirit. She gives birth to the Son of God. Such mythological language would not have seemed exceptional to men and women of the first-century Mediterranean world. Moreover, in Christian tradition, Mary appropriately is given the title "queen of heaven," because of her faithful life. "In Mediterranean Christianity, she also supplies the feminine element missing in a patriarchal religion focused on a patriarchal God."[11] The elevation of Mary continued into the church, once again emphasizing the purity of Mary and the absence of the shame of female bodily functions. More will be discussed in a later chapter.

Christians affirm belief in the power of God through the Holy Spirit to enter into humanity in miraculous ways. Lives are changed through that power. The creation is honored through that power. Love defeats hatred and evil through that power. Mary was obedient to that power in her life as the mother of Jesus.

Throughout history, women, including myself, have participated in the miraculous power of a love that creates new life through the conception and birth of children in the way that God created and called good. We can only wish that all children were created through acts of love. There is no shame in being a woman or man in the human bodies we are given as a gift. Jesus came among us to live as fully human, thus serving as the way God wants us all to live.

If the reason to believe in the virgin birth is that there is something wrong in the human process of sexuality that through love can create life, there are many who cannot accept this reasoning. God created the process of sex, love, and birth. We may continue to discuss and discern in different ways. This is essential to growth in the faith. We need not determine right and wrong in ways that separate believers from one another. Some Scriptures may continue to cause us to question. Perhaps the birth narratives remain in the realm of mystery, with the doctrine of the virgin birth being a way to claim God's agency or to embody Jesus' identity as the Son of God.

More significant is our oneness in the truth and love of the God who has created us and called us good. However we understand the virginity of Mary, that Jesus was born and came among us to embody the creative and unconditional love of God for all humankind is still a miracle. The Christ asks us to live and act in the light of that love.

THE LIFE AND MINISTRY OF JESUS—THE MISFITS

When looking closely at the life and ministry of Jesus, we encounter much that both questions and negates the domination models that had become the law regarding women as sexual property. At the same time, Jesus indicated that he had not come to do away with the Mosaic law. Several authors, writing of Jesus' teaching, preaching, and acts of healing, suggest that the emphasis was on a change in priorities for the faithful.

We will examine many of Jesus' words and actions that highlight the priorities he came to proclaim as God's desire for human life and relationships. Much of what Jesus said and did reflect a partnership model, with all persons seeking to live and witness to the power of God's love. This is reflected in every part of Jesus' life as he again and again spoke of what is called the kingdom of God or the reign of God on earth. While Jesus directly said little about human sexuality and how to live with integrity as a sexual being, it is still fair to conclude that as he honored the wholeness of persons, he understood that wholeness to include sexuality.

Jesus is often referred to as the human face of God, embodying the nature of God who seeks relationship with creation and humanity. We are also aware that powerful segments of the society of his day rejected his message and sought to end his ministry. He spoke and lived the truth in a way that threatened religious and political power structures, and eventually they colluded to kill him. We need to understand what Jesus was saying and doing if we are to follow Christ today.

Jesus challenged the family institution in several ways. The Gospel of Matthew reports that the authorities challenged Jesus on the meaning of divorce (Matthew 19:1–10). In this day of frequent divorce, we might not be satisfied with Jesus' answer to the Pharisees who were seeking to discredit him. We must examine what he said for its deeper meaning.

The law understood a wife to be the property of her husband. Deuteronomy 24:1–4 says that if a husband finds something objectionable about his wife, then he is permitted to write her a bill of divorce. This was final; she had no recourse. There was no discussion of the possibility of a wife divorcing her husband.

The Pharisees cite Moses as the lawgiver. Jesus goes back to the creation story, saying that in the beginning God made them male and female and in marriage they become one. Oneness implies partnership in relationship and sexual love. No one should separate them (Matthew 19:1–12). He allows for divorce if the cause is unchastity, but adds that the husband becomes an adulterer if he divorces for any other reason.

In Mark 10:12, Jesus also indicates the same if a wife divorces her husband.[12] This is the part that must have seemed outrageous to many who heard that slant on the law. Jesus goes back to the creation story where man and woman are equally created in God's image and affirms that women as well as men should not enter into divorce, as the marriage bond is sacred. Integrity within a covenant relationship becomes the priority in God's design. This, of course, includes sexual faithfulness between marriage partners.

Jesus also questions the rigid rules regarding family when he blesses children (Matthew 19:13–15). When the disciples told him to send children away, they were doing what family structure affirmed. Although it was necessary for a woman to produce sons to carry on the family name and heritage, children were low on the hierarchical ladder, often considered a nuisance. Jesus drew them close and blessed them. Today both the Jewish and Christian faiths teach us that doing God's will includes the care and nurture of family life.

One teaching that most affects the understanding of sexual behavior is reported in Matthew 5:27–28. Jesus tells men that even to look at a woman with lust is tantamount to committing adultery. He then repeats the teaching on divorce. Although Jesus is clear that adultery is wrong, we learn more as he deals with an actual situation of a woman about to be stoned for being caught in an adulterous situation (John 7:53–8:11).

Scholars have discovered that this story of the woman caught in adultery was inserted into the biblical canon at a later date.[13] The story very likely circulated earlier in the oral tradition. The reason that the account was included in the New Testament later was that Jesus' followers had heard of such an event and believed that it was congruent with what he said and did. His attitude was not to accept the act of adultery as requiring immediate judgment, but to instead minister to the woman who was implicated and would pay with her life and admonish her to sin no more.

The context for this event was that the authorities were once again attempting to discredit the validity of Jesus as a prophet or as one who had authority to speak for God. They even stated that no prophet was to arise from Galilee (John 7:52). When Jesus returns to the Temple the next morning, the people gather to hear him teach. Some of the Pharisees bring in a woman caught in the act of adultery. They remind him that according to the law she should be stoned. If Jesus fails to agree with them, he could be charged by religious authorities for defying the faith.

What happened next is well known. Jesus bent down and wrote on the ground. They continued to question him, demanding a response. He stood up and said, "Let anyone among you who is without sin be the first to throw a stone at her" (John 8:7b). He bent again, writing on the ground. They went away, beginning with the elders.

When Jesus stood up, only the woman was there. He asked her where her accusers were and if any of them had condemned her. She replied that no one had. He then said to her, "Neither do I condemn you. Go, and from now on do not sin again" (John 8:11).

Jesus is clear in several instances in Scripture that adultery is wrong; it is a sin because it is breaking a relationship. Yet, God's forgiveness is more powerful than sin. As a forgiven woman, she has a second chance to go her way into a future that has new possibilities. Jesus knew that women were often victims in sexual situations. His compassion saved her life and asked her to examine her life in new ways. We will never know the whole story. Was she married? Was he? Were they consenting adults or could she have been forced into the act? Remember in Deuteronomy 22:23–24 a woman had to cry out if she was not to be considered an adulteress. If she did, did anyone hear her?

We also note that there is no mention of the man who was also guilty of adultery. The adulterous man was not part of the judgment as the story is told—nor is he offered Jesus' compassion.

There are other stories of Jesus' interaction with women that batter away at the walls of the entrenched patriarchy. All three Synoptic Gospels contain the story of the woman who had been suffering from hemorrhages for twelve years (Mark 5:25–34, Matthew 9:20–22, Luke 8:43-48). The accounts attest to the fact that she had sought healing from physicians and had spent all she had trying to get well. Mark says that she was in fact getting worse.

She must have already known of the healing power of Jesus for she says, perhaps to herself, "If I can but touch his clothes, I will be made well"

(Mark 5:28). Given the purity codes of Jewish law, this woman had been unclean for all twelve years. A flow of blood always meant that one had to go through the ritual baths to be restored to the community in good standing. Thus she was an outsider among her own people.

I have always imagined her moving through the crowd until she was at his back. She throws herself on her knees and just manages to take hold of the fringe of his outer robe. She experiences the cessation of her flow of blood just as Jesus perceives that power has flowed from him and asks, "Who touched me?" (Luke 8:45a).

No one nearby reports having seen the woman touch his robe. Only she can come forward and identify herself. She is frightened. She trembles. What will he say to her for the audacious thing she has done? Despite her fear, she tells him and the crowd what has just happened and how Jesus has healed her. Jesus then says to her, "Daughter, your faith has made you well; go in peace" (Luke 8:48).

Jesus identifies her faith as a source of the healing that has taken place. This is said often in the healing stories, and is a significant part of the teaching that accompanies the healing. Jesus is telling us that God's grace within us is a part of the healing process of body, mind, and spirit. His power flowed into the woman and ignited her own power to believe and break free of what had become a source of shame and disgrace. Of course, she would have gone through the process of purification before she was once again a part of her community, but the difference was Jesus and the loving power she received. Jesus did not see this woman as one whose sexual functioning had gone awry, but as a person who needed healing to be restored to wholeness.

The beginning of Luke 8 records that in Jesus' travels throughout the region he was accompanied by the twelve disciples and some women who had been cured of evil spirits and infirmities. Several of these women are named, including Mary Magdalene from whom seven demons had been banished. Some of the women might well have suffered in ways similar to the woman who had hemorrhaged for twelve years. Who knows how many of these women were seen as misfits in society? Mary Magdalene has often been characterized as a prostitute, but this is doubtful. Seven demons may have more closely described mental illness of some sort. Mental illness could easily become a reason to describe a person as an outcast. Yet, in the power of God's love through Jesus, they became courageous, spiritually growing persons, ready to share their faith in their world.

Luke records in the previous chapter the incident of the woman who broke into the meal at the Pharisee's house and wept as she anointed Jesus' feet and dried them with her hair. In Luke's Gospel she is cited as a sinner. While no specific sin is mentioned, it is often inferred that this woman was a prostitute (Luke 7:37). The guests most likely were aware of her sin. Jesus speaks of her many sins, recognizing that he was made ritually unclean by her washing his feet. The emphasis here is the lack of the Pharisee's hospitality and the woman's willingness to risk everything to anoint Jesus' feet. Jesus points out her thankfulness for forgiveness in contrast to the failure of the host to provide water for the washing of feet and the expectation of a kiss from host to guest. He says to her again, "Your sins are forgiven" (Luke 7:48). The guests are shocked. He speaks to her with the same words he said to the woman with the flow of blood, "Your faith has saved you; go in peace" (Luke 7:50). A significant part of the change in emphasis Jesus brings is that this woman is given credit for her faith. Jesus, as with the woman caught in adultery, does not condone the prostitution. He simply moves through it to the desire of God to forgive, so that the person can move on into a new future.

John's Gospel says that the woman was Mary, the sister of Lazarus (John 12:1–8). There is no indication that Mary, the sister of Martha and Lazarus, was a prostitute. Mary, Martha, and Lazarus were good friends who had invited Jesus to their home in Bethany. Both stories center on the love of the woman for Jesus' ministry and her willingness to risk everything to honor him.

The story of Jesus' encounter with a Samaritan woman is found in John 4. Many of us learned in Sunday school of the mutual hatred between Jews and Samaritans. This was usually taught in the context of the parable of the good Samaritan, who picked up a wounded traveler and helped him while his own people passed by.

Since Samaritans failed to follow the Jewish laws of purity, the Jews believed that they were not among the chosen people of Israel. Jews were to avoid Samaritans. This is the background to John 4:3–4 as Jesus and the disciples travel back to Galilee. It seems the reason was that Jesus was tired and they went through Samaritan territory, a more direct route. The disciples go off to buy food and a tired Jesus sits by Jacob's well. This story is about walls and how Jesus broke them down.

The first wall is the sharing of theological truth with a woman, likely uneducated in the understanding of spiritual matters, and a Samaritan at that. Jesus engages her fully in a discussion of living water that encourages her to want what he describes to her as a possibility of eternal, abundant life in the Spirit. When she asks questions, he takes her seriously as a partner in the discussion.

The second broken wall relates to the woman's sexual history. He asks her to call her husband. The reader is suspicious that he knows the truth about her situation. She answers that she has no husband. Jesus does know and reveals that he is aware that she has had five husbands and is currently living with a man to whom she is not married. We might surmise that the woman might have had little control over her decision to marry five men. As *The People's New Testament Commentary* suggests, she might have been passed around at the death of her husbands.[14] She is not a respectable woman in her community. Nevertheless, once said, her marital status is not mentioned again. Jesus seems to have a more important agenda than concentrating attention on her sexual past or present. She is so amazed she blurts out that he must be a prophet, and the theological discussion continues. They talk about the different ways they worship.

When John's Gospel was written, perhaps around the year CE 100, the temple at Mount Gerizim in Samaria, like the temple in Jerusalem, had been destroyed. Jesus says that true worship is not in a physical place. It is in receiving the God who came in Jesus Christ. Much of the discussion between the Samaritan woman and Jesus relates to the early Christian community that would have read this story post-Easter, as we read it now.

Her faith leads her to speak of her hope in the coming of the Messiah. He reveals himself as the one. When the disciples return with the food, they are amazed that he is talking to this woman. The woman becomes the first evangelist. She, in her new life of faith and courage, goes into the village and witnesses to her encounter with the Christ. As we leave the narrative, they are seeking to know Jesus.

This story breaks down the walls between people, cultures, ethnicities, religions, and the judgment of persons who, in the eyes of many then and now, have questionable sex lives. Jesus once again sees the whole person and breaks down the wall that separates people into good and bad, the divide that often occurs in regard to sexual behavior. He shows respect for this woman as he engages her in a discussion of the meaning of faith. The misfit wall is broken. The gender wall is broken. It cannot be denied that Jesus casts doubt on the traditional and patriarchal structure throughout his brief earthly ministry, as these stories of his healing and teaching among women testify.

Jesus even allowed a Canaanite woman to tell him that God's healing and grace extended beyond the Jewish people (Matthew 15:21–28). I have participated in many discussions that have considered the possibility that this persistent woman may have played a part in persuading Jesus that his ministry was not limited to the chosen people of Israel. She had one thing on her mind. Her daughter was possessed by a demon. She somehow knew that Jesus could put her in touch with the God who cared about the child. Jesus tries to tell her that he has been sent to the lost sheep of Israel. She kneels before him and begs for help. He answers that the children's food should not be thrown to the dogs. She comes back at him once more as she says that the dogs often eat the crumbs from the master's table, as all dog owners know that dogs are happy to do. Jesus is amazed at her confidence in God's love. He says to her, "Woman, great is your faith! Let it be done for you as you wish" (verse 28). Jesus affirmed her and her desperate love for her daughter in this healing act.

While not related to sexuality as such, Jesus once again demonstrates equality and respect for women in this incident. The implication is that women as well as men are created in God's image, including their sexuality, and are meant to grow in relationship to God who seeks a vibrant relationship with all creation.

Jesus spoke, told stories (parables), and demonstrated a new way of being a person of faith. As Jesus affirmed the equal worth of women, he was also sharing a vision of a God-filled man as one who could share compassion, tenderness, and love of family. He was all of these and strong enough to give his life for what he came to proclaim. While he, as a faithful Jewish person, followed the essentials of his own faith, he also entered into relationships with those who were considered inferior. Outsiders disparaged or ignored by the righteous people were proclaimed as special to God. Women were treated as partners in faith—agents of their own journey in faith and recipients of healing and forgiveness and new life.

He pointed the way to a vision of the kingdom or reign of God that included everyone. It is no wonder that after his death and resurrection, the birthing of the church began with a gathering during the Feast of Weeks that included the Holy Spirit, symbolized by divided tongues of fire resting on each of the gathered men and women as they began to speak in many languages. The living spirit of Christ would come down at Pentecost, and the church would be born.

Endnotes

1. Lester Grabbe, "Seleucid Empire," in *The New Interpreter's Dictionary*, Katherine Doob Sakenfield ed., (Nashville: Abingdon Press, 2009), 5:159.

2. Lester Grabbe, "Hasmoneans," in *The New Interpreter's Dictionary*, 2:740.

3. Jewish Women's Archives, homepage, accessed July 6, 2015, www.jwa.org.

4. Boring, M. Eugene, and Craddock, Fred B., *The People's New Testament Commentary* (Louisville: Westminster John Knox Press, 2004), 14.

5. Margaret Y. McDonald, "Marriage, New Testament," in *The New Interpreter's Dictionary*, 3:813.

6. Mary F. Faskett, "Virgin," in *The New Interpreter's Dictionary*, 5:785.

7. Joel B. Green, "Virgin Birth," in *The New Interpreter's Dictionary*, 5:788.

8. Isaiah 7:14 uses the Hebrew *almah,* meaning "young woman." Matthew 1:23 quotes the Greek version, using *partheonos,* meaning "virgin."

9. Jennifer Wright Knust, *Unprotected Texts: The Bible's Surprising Contradictions About Sex and Desire* (New York: HarperOne, 2011), 231.

10. Michael Coogan, *God and Sex: What the Bible Really Says,* 39.

11. Ibid., 181.

12. Under Jewish law only the husband could initiate a divorce. Mark 10:12, which assumes that a wife could divorce her husband, implies a Greco-Roman setting, where Roman law would apply.

13. Bruce Metzger, *A Textual Commentary on the Greek New Testament* (New York: United Bible Societies, 1975), 219–220.

14. M. Eugene Boring and Fred B. Craddock, *The People's New Testament Commentary,* 300.

CHAPTER 3

The Early Church, St. Paul and Beyond

In his brief time on earth, Jesus returned the essence of faith to the original vision of creation that was called good. He interacted with humanity made in the image of God. Through the incarnation of God in Christ, Jesus lived and died so that all people might live lives of wholeness in every facet of their being and in their relationships. Wholeness of being could only be fulfilled in receiving the gift of God, given in grace.

This image of God in humanity was meant for every part of life, including the gift of sexuality. Old Testament scholar Bruce Birch, in *To Love as We Are Loved*, uses the familiar word "Shalom" as he speaks of wholeness, "Shalom is best understood when we as human beings experience wholeness and harmony with God, with self, with others, and with creation."[1]

Given the many times that Jesus taught, witnessed, demonstrated, and explained again what his coming was about, it is surprising that even after the resurrection, his disciples did not fully understand his ministry. It is no less surprising that we still have the same difficulty.

THE BIRTH OF THE CHURCH—PENTECOST

Jesus made a promise to that community of men and women as he prepared to leave his earthly presence. The Holy Spirit was to come upon them, the very Spirit of God in Christ, energizing them and making of them a body of Christ that would come to be called the church. There is more than one reference to the event we call Pentecost.

John's account testifies that the promise of the Holy Spirit was fulfilled. Jesus appears to the disciples on the evening of the resurrection, saying, "Peace be with you. As the Father has sent me, so I send you." He then breathes on them, saying, "Receive the Holy Spirit. If you forgive the sins of any, they are forgiven them; if you retain the sins of any, they are retained" (John 20:21–23).

In Acts 2 we read the familiar account of the gathering of the faithful together in a house as the Holy Spirit comes among them with tongues as of fire above each. They were then filled with the Holy Spirit and began to speak in the many languages of the Jews from many lands who were present in Jerusalem. Later, they spill out into the crowds outside and Peter addresses them, witnessing to the coming of Jesus, his life, death, and resurrection (Acts 2). The Acts account includes many people who hear and respond to Christ and are baptized. Jesus has already bodily ascended in Acts 1. Their newfound faith has been a gift of the Holy Spirit.

This is so for us as well. This is why we celebrate the birth of the church in the Pentecost event of Acts 2. The ministry of Jesus had already included Gentiles to whom he had affirmed that their faith had made them well. Perhaps the Gentiles were not clear as to Jesus being the Messiah of the Jews, but they knew him as one who came from God and was for them the incarnation of the God who had shown them grace.

THE EXPANDING MINISTRY TO GENTILES

It was not long before the fledgling church had to deal with Gentiles who came from other traditions and now found that Christ was central to their faith. In Acts 10, we read the amazing experience of Peter and Cornelius. Peter enters the home of a Gentile, given direction by the Holy Spirit. Jewish persons who have accompanied Peter are amazed that the Spirit was poured out on the Gentiles just as the Spirit had come to the circumcised. Peter declares that there is no impediment to these new believers being baptized.

A key dispute that arose in the early church concerned circumcision. Little is said about other purity codes that involved women. Yet it does seem clear that there were male leaders in the Jerusalem church that insisted that it was necessary for believers to be circumcised and to follow the law. "It is necessary for them to be circumcised and ordered to keep the law of Moses"(Acts 15:5). The Council at Jerusalem was a significant event in that it was decided to send a letter to Gentile believers exempting them from all Jewish regulations, including circumcision, except eating food offered to idols, from blood, from what is strangled, and from fornication (Acts 15:29). The early church was trying to catch up with the amazing work of the Holy Spirit!

THE EMERGING MINISTRY
OF SAUL/PAUL

Both Peter and Paul had been a part of the Jerusalem council. The story of the early church now moves to Paul, to his dramatic experience on the road to Damascus in Acts 9, and to his mission to the Gentile world. Paul was formerly intent on his mandate as a Pharisee to root out and discipline the new believers in Jesus as the Messiah.

Acts tells us of his zealous actions regarding people faithful to Christ. (They were not called Christians until later.) He had asked the high priest for letters that would authorize him to arrest and bring men and women who were followers of Jesus to Jerusalem. The ninth chapter of Acts tells the dramatic story of Saul's conversion. Later Saul (as he was known in his Jewish community; he was known in Greek-speaking circles by his Greco-Roman name, Paul) begins his missionary enterprises, going first to the synagogues. Starting with Chapter 13, Acts is largely Paul's story as the one who is sent to the Gentile community, often because he and his companions are forced from the synagoguesby leaders who consider the message of Christ to be blasphemy.

Many of us have studied the missionary journeys of Paul over the years in Sunday school and Bible classes. As churches began to form in the places Paul spread the gospel, he began to write letters to the churches he couldn't visit regularly. It is in these letters that we encounter his theology, his vision for the church, and issues of sexuality within the budding Christian communities.

There are Christian believers today who rely literally on the teachings in Paul's letters. Other contemporary Christians dismiss Paul as not authoritative for faith formation, especially as the faith addresses the status of women and of sexuality. Maxine Beach in her 1999 study *The Bible – The Book that Bridges the Millennia*, says, "Although we affirm diversity, and the early church did welcome Jew and Gentile, male and female, slave and free, church history has included conflict and division."[2] There continues to be division within the body of Christ today, based on issues of interpretation and authority of Scripture. Perhaps it is important to see Paul as an intense man, caught at times in a battle for a faith that changed not only his life, but also the lives of Gentiles and Jews throughout the world of his day. There are times when he may be inconsistent, falling back on the culture from which he came, and other times when he forges new paths for the growing community of faith in Jesus.

Like Jesus, Paul at times was willing to sublimate rules and culture for the church that believed in and practiced the saving power of Jesus Christ. New Testament scholar L. William Countryman says, "The great issue of conversion for Paul, then, was not whether to keep the law, but whether to rely on it. Once he had become convinced that he must rely on another source of righteousness, he was no longer tied to the law, but could use it or not in accordance with the now dominant concerns associated with the 'righteousness that comes through Christ's faith.'"[3]

Countryman refers to 1 Corinthians 9:19–23 where Paul states that, while he is free from the law, he follows it among Jewish believers in order to witness to Christ. He can also refrain from the law when among Gentiles for the same purpose. "To the weak, I became weak, so that I might win the weak.

I have become all things to all people that I might by all means save some. I do it for the sake of the gospel, so that I may share in its blessings" (1 Corinthians 9:22–23). Such a practice would have made a difference to Gentiles who came to the faith outside the purity codes of the law.

There are other facets of Paul's views on sexuality that have long been under discussion in Christian communities. In 1 Corinthians 5, Paul speaks of sexual immorality that, if continued, will defile the community. A man is living with his father's wife, something not to be countenanced. Paul goes on to speak of other immoral practices. The Greek word *porneia* is used to cover several sorts of immoral behavior. Its meaning covers illicit sexual acts such as adultery, sex with animals, and incest, but it can also include worship of idols.[4] In 1 Corinthians 6:12, Paul uses what is called a maxim, a saying that gets to the heart of the matter. Such sayings were popular in Greco-Roman education and culture. "'All things are lawful for me,' but not all things are beneficial."

This gives rise to Paul's discussion of behavior that can denigrate or uplift the community. Sexual behavior and practice are included. 1 Corinthians 7 is a long treatise on marriage, very likely an answer to questions that had arisen in the church. Paul begins by saying that a man should not touch a woman. This is another maxim, which exists to guard against immorality (*porneia*). Therefore, Paul says that a man should have his own wife and a woman her own husband. Paul is defending monogamy.

He then goes on to state that each person in a marriage has authority over the body of the other and owes conjugal rights to the marriage partner. They can by mutual consent refrain from sex for a time to devote more time to prayer, but they are not to refrain from intercourse if tempted beyond their self-control. This is an explicit instruction given to married persons in the church with the understanding that sexual desire is a part of being human.

It is also important to remember that most people in the ancient world did not understand hormones and bodily functions as we do in contemporary culture. Paul goes on to lift up his own decision to be celibate and offers that state to widows, the unmarried, and virgins. He also suggests that in case of separation or divorce, celibacy is the best option.

The very early Christians believed that Christ would return very soon, and that it was the life of prayer and witness that was the most desirable mode of life in preparation for Jesus' return. This is discussed in Paul's letters; the earliest reference to the *parousia*, which is the word for coming or arrival used in 1 Thessalonians 4. In this early letter, Paul speaks in the first twelve verses of the manner of life the community should be living. In verse 13, he continues to focus on the coming of the Lord. Too much time spent on sexual concerns could get in the way of this imminent return of Jesus. At the same time, Paul is practical as 1 Corinthians 7 evidences. He does have some understanding of sexual passion and desire. 1 Corinthians 7:36–39 speaks of engaged persons. If the passions are strong, they should get married, but refraining from marriage is better.

In Chapter 11 of 1 Corinthians, Paul acknowledges equal rights in marriage to women and men. This negates the concept that a wife is only the property of her husband. At the same time, he follows the earlier theology that Christ is the head of the man and husbands the head of wives (1 Corinthians 11:3). However, later in the same chapter, Paul points to a less hierarchical understanding, "For just as woman came from man, so man comes through woman; but all things come from God" (verse 12). Paul acknowledges the birth process here in a powerful sense by pointing out that all human life comes from God through the womb.

This is the same Paul who states in Galatians 3:28–29, "There is no longer Jew or Greek, there is no longer slave or free, there is no longer male or female; for all of you are one in Christ Jesus. And if you belong to Christ, then you are Abraham's offspring, heirs according to the promise."

At times, Paul seems to fall back on his old interpretations. Paul was human and like all of us was a person of his culture and context. At the same time, he is able to forge ahead with new understandings as God is revealed to him. Perhaps these new insights are in part due to the leadership of the women he encountered in the development of the church. He cites several of these women in his letters. Lydia, a businesswoman, offered her home to Paul for a church. Priscilla, a learned woman, was equal in witness with her husband, Aquila. In Romans 16, Paul greets Phoebe, a deacon in the church at Cenchreae that also included Priscilla and Aquila. He cites Junia, who with others was in prison with him. He admonishes Euodia and Syntyche, two women of the church in Philippi who worked with Paul and are likely dear friends, to settle the dispute between them.

INFLUENCES IN PAUL'S TEACHING

Paul was not the first person in history whose writings may appear inconsistent to some of us. The tradition says that Paul came from Tarsus, a city of Hellenistic, Roman, and Jewish culture. He was also a faithful Jew. He would have understood and written in Greek, even as he knew Hebrew. He was likely influenced by his culture, study of Scripture, and new experiences in establishing churches among the Gentiles. Inconsistency in the interpretation of Scripture still exists. In the 1960s, a group of us in church leadership were discussing the disconnection between the emerging acceptance of women as leaders, both lay and clergy, and the ongoing elevation of sermons and Bible studies about the Scriptures that insist on the submission of wives, daughters, and widows. In some places, this discussion is still going on.

We had experienced men and women cautioning women to think hard about answering a call to ordained ministry. One prominent male pastor said to me when I mentioned my plan to go to seminary, "Whatever you do, don't hurt your husband." My husband and I later served as a clergy couple, faithful to the ministry of the church and to each other. Six years after his death I met, fell in love with, and married another clergyman.

Laywomen from our group were encountering resistance from male leadership as they began to contribute more of their time and talent to the ministries of the church. A workshop facilitator reminded us that we were living in a crucial time in history: the image of being born female was changing. Women were emerging as strong, talented, creative, and ready to partner with men in working to make God's vision of justice, peace, and equality a more present reality. At the same time, she said, change is often countered with stiff resistance from those who feel better if everything remains as it was. Fear of change was nothing new in Paul's time, nor is it in our contemporary world.

Another hot issue in the interpretation of Paul's writings refers to many references to human life as lived in the flesh and in the spirit. In Paul's time, other religions and philosophies in the surrounding cultures assumed a dualism of "flesh" and "spirit." They were seen as two distinct facets of human nature.

If a dualistic approach is accepted, it is easy to apply definitions to both that suggest opposites. Further, it then becomes possible to label "spirit" as good and "flesh" (body) as bad. Paul takes great pains so that his readers will understand the relationship between the two categories. Flesh can indeed refer to the physical aspect of our humanity. Paul acknowledges that the body is a part of God's creation. "Do you not know that your bodies are members of Christ?" (1 Corinthians 6:15a). He also believed that temptation could quickly arise if the flesh were without the spirit. In Romans 8, there is extensive discussion of his belief that living by the dictates of the flesh alone can result in sin, which can lead to death. By death, he means opposition to God and to God's spirit in us. "For this reason the mind that is set on the flesh is hostile to God; it does not submit to God's law—indeed it cannot, and those who are in the flesh cannot please God" (Romans 8:7–8).

The danger that has come from this interpretation is that for many the sins of the flesh have come to be related to sexual sin alone. This is not true to Paul. *The Interpreter's Dictionary of the Bible* reminds us that living "according to the flesh, '*kata sarka*' in Greek, covers many human temptations such as envy, acquisitiveness, self-satisfaction."[5] Flesh (*sarx* in Greek) can refer to the wider sphere of sinfulness, to the entire personality wrongly directed.

Paul believed that the Gentiles who came into the Christian faith had not had the benefit of life in the spirit before coming to receive God's grace in Christ. In this sense, they had been more vulnerable to the flesh, including questionable sexual practices. At the same time, he was critical of the Jewish faithful who practiced the law without the spirit. He does not negate the physical needs or desires of living in a body, despite his belief that the *parousia* or end time was near. It is clear that, for Paul, life in Christ was the harmony of the body and the spirit. Life in the flesh was made whole by the Spirit, and the Spirit was God's presence in every aspect of the life of the one who was in Christ.

DEUTERO-PAULINE AND OTHER WRITINGS IN THE NEW TESTAMENT

It has become clear to many biblical scholars that some of the letters attributed to Paul were letters that bore his name, but were crafted by those who knew and honored Paul's work. A term for such work, reflecting a famous and honored writer but written by someone else, is "Deutero." *The People's New Testament Commentary* suggests that 1 Thessalonians, 1 Corinthians, Philemon, Philippians, 2 Corinthians, Galatians, and Romans are undisputed as authentic Pauline letters. The authorship of others such as Colossians, Ephesians, and 2 Thessalonians is more questionable.[6] Many scholars believe that the pastoral letters, 1 and 2 Timothy and Titus, were written later, but reflected Paul, their apostolic leader. Writing something and then ascribing what was written to a famous and influential leader was not considered plagiarism in the ancient world. Writers often used a famous name to highlight their work and to pay respect.

Years ago, my husband and I taught the spiritual growth study on Ephesians. We decided to stage a brief debate as to whether Ephesians was the work of Paul or the work of one of his disciples. Our purpose was to indicate that scholars are not always agreed on historical facts. My husband believed that Paul did write Ephesians, and I was more persuaded that someone else had written the letter. Specific dates for the letters are hard to find. We had a lively time, discussing in a friendly spirit. The debate was conducted to encourage those listening not to be afraid to pray, ask questions, discern, study, and interpret Scripture. Great wisdom arises when we come together as seekers for truth in faith and Scripture. I think there is an overarching priority in the Gospels and other New Testament writings on the unity and love binding those who came to know the grace of God through Christ. This is the one imperative; everything else is subordinate.

Before we go further in our exploration of the New Testament and sexuality, a word of caution may be in order. L. William Countryman puts it this way, "This brings me to the other and greater barrier which modern readers must overcome in accepting the New Testament witness on the subject of purity—our own traditional preconceptions. Sex is not a primary concern in the New Testament writings nor is physical purity an accepted principle there. To those who read the New Testament in the light of modern Western Christianity this will always be difficult to comprehend or accept, for a long history of pietism, both Protestant and Catholic, has made physical purity a major principle and sex a primary concern among us."[7] This puts a discussion of the Bible and sexuality in a wider context with the growing church at the center. It is in this light that we examine the later letters and writings of the New Testament.

The Johannine Epistles (1, 2, and 3 John) reframe family altogether as those who are living in the love of Christ. 1 John 3:18 states, "Little children, let us love, not in word or speech, but with truth and action." The author addresses the church members as children who are righteous and cannot sin if they are filled with the love of Jesus Christ. Love is the key to being in Christ. The children are admonished to love one another as Christ loves them. Many pastors, including myself, have often used the exalted love passages from 1 John in wedding ceremonies. One could do well to build a sexual ethic based on 1 John 4. The author asserts that God is love and when we love, we are in God.

Another issue arises when we turn to other letters. One of the reasons many scholars are sure Paul did not write 1 and 2 Timothy or Titus, and that Peter the apostle did not write 1 and 2 Peter, is that those writings reflect the circumstances of a later time. Paul lived approximately from 5–57 CE, while the events of these books take place at a later time. In these books, the church is in the process of becoming more organized, often in response to the Roman culture that surrounded it. The coming of Christ in the *parousia* has not happened in the way it was expected in 1 Thessalonians.

These letters, written toward the end of the first century, urged decorum among Christians as a part of their witness to the pagan world. Rome was a hierarchy headed by the emperor. This had implications for the church as well. These later epistles have several sections in which the instruction echoes patriarchal patterns, which were not taught by Jesus and, in most instances, not by Paul. There are strict implications for sexuality in these instructions. When certain categories of humanity are relegated by leaders (usually male) to a lower status, the very definition of those who are to submit is determined by those in power. Sexuality is a part of that picture, as are the instructions to slaves who are to obey their masters.

In 1 Peter 3, the author tells wives how to behave by indicating how they should dress and how they should, like Sarah, obey their husbands. Husbands, on the other hand, are to pay honor to their wives as they are the "weaker" sex (1 Peter 3:1–7). How long in human history has a literal interpretation of that statement and others like it affected the role of women, including the perception of feminine sexuality? How should we see it?

1 Timothy is largely a letter of instruction to the church about the various offices held by the leaders of the congregations. The specificity indicates several decades of church structure development. The author speaks of the various orders of ministry, bishops and deacons in particular. When he defines the role of women, the author steps far back of the words and practices of Paul and the witness of Jesus Christ. His interpretation could be reflecting the Roman/Greek culture of the time, or it could also reflect the Jewish heritage

that was a part of the early church tradition. Whatever his reasons, male leadership in the church was emphasized.

1 Timothy 2:11–15 is clear in indicating the position of women and the expected function of their sexuality: "Let a woman learn in silence with full submission. I permit no woman to teach or to have authority over a man; she is to keep silent. For Adam was formed first, then Eve; and Adam was not deceived, but the woman was deceived and became a transgressor. Yet she will be saved through childbearing, provided they continue in faith and love and holiness, with modesty." Such a passage reminds us of the admonition to King Ahasuerus by Memucan, one of the king's advisors. Queen Vashti had refused to come at the summons of her husband, the king, when he called her to appear before him at the grand celebration. Memucan declared that the refusal was more than a royal wife saying no to a royal husband. He said to the officials of the court, "For this deed of the queen will be made known to all women, causing them to look with contempt on their husbands" (Esther 1:17a). This of course led to the banishment of Vashti and the choice of Esther as queen.

This is a clear instance of misinterpretation of the story of the Garden of Eden. Maleness is absolved of responsibility for sin and evil entering the world. The woman is at fault and is to be punished. Her only possible virtue is her womb. The only result of intercourse is to give birth to children. There is no provision for the woman unable to bear children, despite story after story of God's grace to barren women. We remember the stories of Sarah, Hannah, Elizabeth, and others. Of course there was no knowledge at the time of infertility in some men. There is no mention of the women leaders in the Hebrew text encountered by Jesus or known and greeted by the church.

The church had moved a long way in these letters from cooperative models of human interaction that offered freedom to all. In 2 Timothy we read the exhortation to shun youthful passions (2 Timothy 2:22). Titus admonishes married women to be self-controlled and chaste, good managers and submissive to their husbands, so that the Word of God may not be discredited (Titus 2:4–5).

It is essential, perhaps especially when we disagree with certain ideas in some passages of Scripture, that we try to understand the context in which they were written and the point of view of the writer. On the other hand, some of these Scriptures reflecting hierarchy, submission, sublimation of passion, silence for women, and in the past, rules for slaves, have been taken quite literally and applied uncritically to today's world. In the name of stability in the church or world, there are those who have reaped great advantages from a world of status where many others silently submit to those in power. We might ask in protest why attention is not given to Scriptures that speak to us about the wonder of all creation and the value of every woman, man, child, and all of the life around us?

This is not to say that organization and leadership are inherently wrong. No one who loves John Wesley could say so. It is a danger in any organization, including the church, that power can and sometimes does become the primary value to those wielding power. The purpose of the writers of the letters mentioned was to build up the church for its witness to the world. The church was meant to reflect the love of Christ as the body of Christ, sent to those who needed to hear and receive the gospel message. Yet, at times there were those who succumbed to the lure of power and justified their misuse of power by claiming authorization given by God in Scripture. This tendency has not disappeared.

The scriptural weight of the letter of James has often been discounted, even by reformer Martin Luther. As *The People's New Testament Commentary* observes, "James has suffered among Christian readers, especially Protestants, since Luther's unfortunate reference to it as 'a rather strawy epistle.'"[8] Yet James reflects the witness of the heart changed by faith and works as they are in harmony with each other. The tone is different from the previous authors: "So speak and so act as those who are to be judged by the law of liberty. For judgment will be without mercy to anyone who has shown no mercy; mercy triumphs over judgment" (James 2:12–13).

Along with Hebrew Scripture writers and with Matthew, James speaks of Rahab, the Gentile prostitute who was justified when she welcomed the Hebrew messengers and helped them to escape. Rahab was declared right by God because of her good deeds, despite the usual reactions to her profession. Her works testified to her faith. James states, "For just as the body without the spirit is dead, so faith without works is also dead" (James 2:26).

The Letter to the Hebrews is a very different book, with the major emphasis on the sacrifice of Jesus, which supplants the old sacrificial system. Jesus, unblemished, gave himself as a sacrifice for the sins of all, past and present. The Christology of Hebrews names Jesus as a high priest, reflecting temple worship. The writer claims the tradition of the sacred priesthood, a male tradition, for Jesus. Christians are to live in the light of that gift of God, and to submit to their leaders.

Hebrews does not suggest different responsibilities for men and women when it comes to marriage. Its only instruction is to hold marriage in honor and keep the marriage bed undefiled, as God will judge fornicators and adulterers.

The author of Hebrews declines to name the status and duties of categories of persons who are part of the church, as his or her priority is to claim Christ as all that we need to purify ourselves and to approach God, cleansed and forgiven. "Let us approach with a true heart in full assurance of faith, with our hearts sprinkled clean from an evil conscience and our bodies washed with pure water" (Hebrews 10:22).

The final book of the New Testament continues to lend itself to myriad interpretations and many questions. The imagery in Revelation has been both used and misused from the time it was written until the present day as indicators of what will happen in terms of world events.

What we do know is that the book was likely written between CE 80 and 100. This was a time when some Christians were assimilating into the Roman culture, which insisted that all people acknowledge the emperor as a god.

Many Christians sought to find a compromise between faith and Roman culture. Such assimilation also offered Christians opportunities to succeed in the world of commerce, a diverse world as to culture.[9]

To John of Patmos, this was an anathema. There are two points that tie his anger with idolatry and sex. These are related to Paul's discussion of the flesh. The earthly part of a human, if not balanced with the spiritual nature, could lead to sin. Sin could consist of temptations, including unacceptable sexual behavior, greed, failure to maintain courage in the face of persecution, and many others.

The first few chapters of Revelation introduce admonitions to seven churches. In the message to Pergamum, John cites those who are following the teaching of Balaam. This teacher has told them it is acceptable to eat food offered to idols. The writer condemns this and the practice of fornication, which in Greek is the same word often used for sexual immorality (Revelation 2:12–17).

In the letter to Thyatira, the writer invokes the name of Jezebel, who is leading the congregation astray. This refers back to Jezebel in 1 Kings, who married Ahab, king of Israel, and influenced him to establish Baal worship in Israel.

John says she refuses to repent of her fornication. As a result, she will be thrown on a bed and there are those who will commit adultery with her. The adulterers will be in great distress unless they repent. Her children will be struck dead.

Another message is given to the church in Laodicea when they are told that they are to be spit from God's mouth for their failure to be zealous in their witness; they are "neither hot nor cold" (Revelation 3:16). They do not know that they are "wretched, pitiable, poor, blind, and naked" (Revelation 3:17b). They are to buy white robes to cover the shame of their nakedness. This sense of shame about the human body goes back centuries. It goes forward, also.

There are other sexual images in Revelation that point beyond themselves to the primary points that John seeks to make. It is his use of vivid sexual imagery that illustrates the message. In Revelation 12 he presents a woman from heaven, pregnant and crying out in birth pangs. A dragon awaits the birth in order to devour the child. She gives birth to a son who is snatched away and taken to the throne of God, and the woman flees to the wilderness where she is nourished for 1,260 days.

The People's New Testament Commentary suggests that the original readers were familiar with the language and imagery of Revelation. "John himself and most of his original readers recognized this type of language as a powerful vehicle for communicating the divine message already found in the Bible and in several streams of Judaism. Apocalyptic writings were already present in John's Bible (e.g., Isa. 24–27; Daniel 7–12)."[10]

The New Interpreter's Dictionary suggests that much of the imagery in Revelation has to do with the oppression of Rome over the people Rome had conquered, now including Christian churches.[11] Rome is Babylon and will, according to John, ultimately be destroyed. He presents in Chapter 17 and following the great whore, a woman clothed in scarlet and purple, adorned with jewels and holding a golden cup full of the abominations and the impurities of her fornication. In fact, she is called the mother of whores. She rules at present, but will be destroyed in the end. Interestingly, the Jewish Annotated New Testament suggests, "The earliest uses of Revelation understood it as unrelated to any particular historical context. In second-century Asia Minor and third-century Upper Egypt, for example, the book was read as sanction for an imminent millennium on earth." Generations since have persisted in interpreting Revelation in light of contemporary historical events. Blood and suffering suggested martyrdom.[12] Once again, interpretations can vary greatly depending on the culture, theology, and history of the interpreters.

Continuing with the imagery, after the destruction, the New Jerusalem will come from heaven as a bride adorned for her husband. Of course, such a bride would be a virgin, the image of purity. Perhaps this is just one of the places that have given rise to what we have come to call "the virgin/whore syndrome." Women have often been stifled by this image. A woman must be one or the other, a pure and nearly sexless being or a wild woman, ready for sex with anyone at any time.

The other strange sexual imagery in Revelation comes with the often-discussed 144,000 who are sealed as presented in Chapter 7. There are 12,000 from each of the tribes who carry the seal on their foreheads. In Chapter 14, the 144,000 are said to be those redeemed from humankind as first fruits for God and the Lamb. The name of God is on their foreheads. Only they could learn the harpist's song. They are all male virgins who have not defiled themselves with women. The author here is speaking of ritual defilement or some other form of impurity. They follow the Lamb and are blameless. The intent of John of Patmos is often hard to detect. At times, the images take on meanings of their own, lending themselves to broad varieties of interpretation.

All in all, John of Patmos fears for the life and witness of the church in a time of persecution. He fears that Christians will give in to Rome's demands and the faith will be diluted or die. These are not insignificant concerns, then or now. Revelation is not about sexuality per se; sexual imagery is used to get at John's meaning. There are those who would interpret that imagery in ways that harm the image of the whole person, created by God as both flesh and spirit, held together by the love of Jesus Christ.

The New Testament is always finally about Jesus the Christ. He loved and ministered to all who would receive him. He reminded us that, in the reign of God, the first would be last. Status and hierarchy were not of great importance to him. This must help us to shape our understanding of sexuality for ourselves and for others. L. William Countryman wrote, ". . . modern" Christians find it hard to believe that the New Testament writers were, in fact, ethically indifferent to what we would call 'dirty' behavior and that they adopted this stance of indifference in response to the demands of the gospel itself. If the gospel is indeed 'God's power for salvation to everyone who believes' (Romans 1:16), then it must welcome the leper, the menstruant, the uncircumcised Gentile, indeed all the unclean without exception."[13] Given many of the New Testament teachings that led later to theology that denigrated the sexual aspects of humanity, we might do well to review the creation narratives, Song of Songs, and the teachings and action of Jesus the Christ as we reflect on the wholeness of our creation as human persons, sexuality included.

Endnotes

1. Bruce Birch, *To Love as We Are Loved: The Bible and Relationships* (Nashville: Abingdon Press, 1992), 68.

2. Maxine Beach, *The Bible: The Book that Bridges the Millennia, Part 2: Interpretation and Authority* (New York: The United Methodist Church, General Board of Global Ministries, 1999), vi.

3. L. William Countryman, *Dirt, Greed, and, Sex: Sexual Ethics in the New Testament and Their Implications for Today* (Minneapolis: Fortress Press, 2007), 100.

4. "Porneia," Blue Letter Bible Greek Lexicon, King James Version, Strongs entry G4202, accessed July 15, 2015, www.blueletterbible.org/lang/lexicon/lexicon.cfm?Strongs=G4202&t=KJV.

5. J.D.G. Dunn, "Flesh in the New Testament," in *The New Interpreter's Dictionary*, 2:462.

6. M. Eugene Boring and Fred B. Craddock, *The People's New Testament Commentary*, 467.

7. L. William Countryman, *Dirt, Greed, and Sex*, 141–142.

8. M. Eugene Boring and Fred B. Craddock, *The People's New Testament Commentary*, 714.

9. Craig R. Koester, "Revelation, The Book of," in *The New Interpreter's Dictionary*, 4: 787.

10. M. Eugene Boring and Fred B. Craddock, *The People's New Testament Commentary*, 762.

11. Craig R. Koester, "Revelation, The Book of," in *The New Interpreter's Dictionary*, 4:787.

12. Amy-Jill Levine and Marc Zvi Brettler, *The Jewish Annotated New Testament* (Oxford University Press, 2011), 464.

13. L. William Countryman, *Dirt, Greed, and Sex*, 142.

✳ ✳ ✳ CHAPTER 4

The Church Interprets the Bible

The process of canonization of the New Testament was a long one that continued into the fourth and fifth centuries. The canon is the accepted collection of Scriptures considered authoritative for the church. It is important to know that the Scriptures that became part of the canon did so through the interpretation of church leaders. We will review briefly in this study the process by which interpretations became formative and why these still influence the church in the present.

We concluded Chapter 3 with the witness of the first Christians and the growth of the infant church. We discover an increasingly diverse community of believers in the growth of the early church. We know that there continued to be numbers of Jewish faithful who believed Jesus to be the promised Messiah. They shared faith in Peter's sermon at Pentecost as told in Acts 2:31.

We also know that, early in the life of the church, there were Gentiles of varying ethnic groups. One such Gentile was Lydia, who is described as "a worshiper of God" (Acts 16:14), a quasi-technical term for persons who had not gone through initiatory rites of the Jewish faith and did not keep Mosaic law.[1] The infant church continued to receive persons from many traditions. Much of this growth was due to Paul and his missionary journeys.

The growing membership of the church included people who discovered in Christianity a welcome that provided them status as loved children of God. These persons may have come from a world where their status was denigrated. Some were wealthy Jews. Women were welcomed as equals for a time. Some of the new members were slaves. Others came because of beliefs that had been disparaged in their former communities. In early Christianity they found a status that gave each a respected place in the church.

There was always a strong connection to Judaism from which the church had come. As varieties of Gentiles sought the love of God through Christ, other traditions came with them. We will highlight some that gave rise to major conflicts in the early church.

Greek philosophers such as Socrates, Aristotle, and Plato have been influential throughout history. In Acts 8, we read of Simon, later called Simon Magus. Simon was operating in Samaria, seemingly performing miracles of healing. Peter and John go to Samaria to confront Simon, who offers money for the apostles to lay hands on him. The apostles tell Simon that spiritual gifts are not about money but are a gift of God.

Some scholars over the centuries have equated Simon with Gnosticism, a belief system that was in conflict with orthodox or traditional Christianity for centuries. Gnosticism is basically translated as "knowledge." There are aspects of this system that directly impinged on biblical interpretations of sexuality.

At the core of Gnosticism is the view of knowledge as the superior human condition. There is a dualism here. The world of mind and spirit is the realm of God and the Holy Spirit. The lesser world is the material world, which includes the body. Paul, in his discussion of flesh and spirit, did not put the flesh outside the creative love of God. He, as did Jesus through the Jewish tradition, saw humankind as a whole being, flesh and spirit. J.N.D. Kelly in *Early Christian Doctrines* suggests that there were Jewish antecedents of Gnosticism, likely from heterodox sources predating Christianity. These are sources outside the standard, more traditional source material.[2] At any rate, the emphasis in gnostic Christianity is on the spiritual as opposed to the wholeness of created being.

Kelly explains, "The spiritual element yearns for God, and salvation consists in its liberation from the lower elements with which it is united. This is the task which the Savior Jesus accomplishes. According to their constitution, there are three classes of men (and women)—the carnal or material, the psychic and the pneumatic. Those who are carnal cannot in any way be saved, while in order to attain redemption the pneumatic only need to apprehend the teaching of Jesus. The psychic class can be saved, though with difficulty, through the knowledge of Jesus."[3]

Over the years there were different applications of the understanding of the superiority of knowledge or the pneumatic (spirit) over the flesh (material). Some Gnostics believed the flesh to be so evil it must be avoided altogether if possible. This was an attitude that denounced sexuality. Perhaps procreation was at times a necessary evil. Other Gnostics, emphasizing mind and spirit, deemed the material or physical aspect of humanity of no importance. It did not matter what one did with fleshly desire regarding sex or other bodily functions. *The Oxford Guide to the Bible* states, "The evidence of the Nag Hammadi documents, however, suggests while some Gnostics may have shown libertine tendencies, the main direction of the movement was toward asceticism."[4]

In the second century a theologian named Marcion rejected the Hebrew Scriptures and the narratives of Jesus' birth. Church historian Henry Chadwick says, "It was inconceivable that the divine redeemer could ever have been born of a woman, and Marcion rejected the story of the birth and childhood of Christ as a falsification imposed on the authentic story."[5]

Marcion's view therefore excluded all influence of the Jewish tradition on Christianity. This would have excluded the goodness of God's creation of the material world, including human wholeness of body, mind, and spirit, all called good by God. The Marcionite community rejected marriage, as they regarded sex as coming from an inferior creator. Marcion believed the Jewish Christians had completely misinterpreted the Hebrew Bible.[6]

Another expression of Gnosticism was Manicheism, which reached most of the known world for a time. This theology came from Persian Zoroastrian that taught that this world was an ongoing struggle between light and darkness and only turning toward the light or soul could save a person.[7] While we might believe aspects of Gnosticism to be wrong, the Christian Gnostics sought to deal with theological issues such as the problem of evil, the nature of humanity and our human destiny, and the awakening of the human spirit. They, like the more orthodox Christians, sought to faithfully interpret Scripture in light of the coming of Jesus. Particular Scriptures in the canon such as John's Gospel, with its spiritual nature, influenced later Gnostics.

Interpretations of Scripture led to varied writings over the first few centuries of Christianity. Gnosticism produced writings that were thought of as Scripture by Gnostic Christians. There were hints of resistance by traditional Christians in the later books of the New Testament canon such as the pastoral epistles (1 and 2 Timothy and Titus, Jude, and 1 John). Conflict over spirit, mind, and body led to varied interpretations of sexuality, the place of women in the faith, and the freedom of Christians to pray, listen, and discern God's message in Scripture for themselves and for the community.

The authority of Scripture was dealt with in the early church in two main ways. One concerned the Scriptures that first circulated among the churches. First, there was the Hebrew Bible. In Jesus' time, they used a canon likely formed before the second century BCE. There was no organized and accepted New Testament canon at first. Paul's letters became available, as did fragments of the Gospels and other writings. Much of the gospel message was transmitted orally at first.

As mentioned above, the final stage of the New Testament canon was not complete until around the fifth century. We know that even then there were disputes over the Apocryphal/Deuterocanonical books. These are books contained in the Septuagint, a Greek translation of the Hebrew Scriptures that came from Alexandria between 285–246 BCE. There were disputes as well about later books, eventually known collectively as the New Testament Apocrypha. Because the fragments and stories were believed by some to have come from eyewitnesses or apostolic sources, they carried with them divine authority.

The other growing authority came from the leaders of the churches, also believed to be endowed with divine power, to interpret and teach the truth of Scripture in the community. A dear friend of mine, a retired Roman Catholic priest, once reminded me that most of the development of the ecclesiology and ordering of the ministry of the church was patterned after Roman leadership. Those men and women of the early church who were closest to the eyewitnesses of Jesus' ministry or were a part of the early apostolic mission rose into leadership in the churches.

In the later books of the New Testament, we read about bishops, deacons, and elders. Members of the churches were increasingly admonished to obey the authority of their leaders. Hebrews 13:7 says, "Remember your leaders, those who spoke the Word of God to you; consider the outcome of their way of life, and imitate their faith." 1 Timothy 5:17 states, "Let the elders who rule well be considered worth of double honor, especially those who labor in preaching and teaching."

The early church needed unity as it grew in numbers. Rome was a well-ordered state with a law system to keep order, and had ruled for centuries. There were those who considered such order a good thing for the unity of the church. Thus, Scripture as they heard and read it and the leadership of the early churches became authoritative for the first few centuries of Christianity and continues for some into contemporary times.

Despite the unity of authority in Scripture and church leadership, varieties of interpretation of truth persisted. Once again, much of this was due to Gnostic influence; the conflict over the material world and what that implied for the creation of the body and of sexuality. This same argument had much to do with the gradual denigration of women as an equal part of humanity and the partnership of women with men in the developing church.

Around the second century, the orthodox view of the order of the church began to suppress the openness that had existed earlier. Author Diarmaid MacCulloch, a historian, describes the Christian community as exclusive.

Christians did not mix freely with non-Christians, as Christians regarded many non-Christian practices as pagan and some as demonic. MacCulloch states that "Christians cut across the normal courtesies of observing the imperial cult and that made them a potential force for disruption in Rome."[8] A part of this suppression was related to the conflict with Gnostics and the move to ban or destroy books of Scripture considered gnostic by the hierarchy. Some interesting gnostic fragments that apply to the place of women have come to light in modern times.

Author Elaine Pagels has done extensive work on the gnostic gospels in her book of the same title.[9] One such writing is called the Gospel of Mary. Mary Magdalene is lifted up as the disciple that Jesus loved best. She challenges the authority of Peter after the resurrection and ascension of Christ. The other disciples declare that they must listen to her because she was one who understood Christ's message. Pagels says, "With regard to scripture, 'It is the winners who write history their way. No wonder, then, that the viewpoint of the successful majority has dominated all traditional accounts of the origin of Christianity.'" She also states, "But the discoveries at Nag Hammadi reopen fundamental questions concerning scripture."[10]

Ironically, Tertullian, an orthodox church leader around CE 190, was outraged at the equal participation of women in the church. He objected to women discussing theology, curing the sick, and baptizing other women. He also fought against any idea that there might be female aspects to the divine presence.

At around the same time, a Gospel of Thomas appeared with a concluding statement in opposition to any idea of Mary's leadership. "Simon Peter said to them (the disciples): Let Mary leave us, for women are not worthy of Life.' Jesus said, 'I myself shall lead her, in order to make her male, so that she too may become a living spirit, resembling you males. For every woman who will make herself male will enter the Kingdom of Heaven.'"[11] All of this impinges upon later views of the sexuality of women in relationship to men.

Christianity had become the official religion of the realm at the time of Emperor Constantine in the fourth century. Just as Christians pray now for victory in war and peace to follow, many Christians had hoped that Roman order would continue. Despite the persecution of Christians and Jews that had occurred from time to time, there had been many years of stable culture and a growing Christian church. Roman clerics and soldiers had brought Christianity to every country under Roman rule. There were, of course, still pagan religions in many places, but Christianity was in ascendancy.

An event that had wide influence in the Christian community and in the world at large began in the fifth century CE. The Roman Empire had expanded its rule beyond the Mediterranean world into northern Europe. But the empire began to crumble. By this time, the Christian church was established, with a developing imperialism of its own and a growing clerical leadership (male clergy). Diarmaid MacCulloch states, "What was nevertheless now apparent was that the Catholic Church had become an imperial church, its fortunes linked to those of emperors who commanded armies, to sustain and extend their power in the ways armies do."[12]

The worldwide blow to the sense of stability brought about by the attacks on Rome caused the church to deal with some deep theological and scriptural issues. Confidence was shaky now. Who was "Caesar" in the new configuration? Which institutions should Christians honor? What were the implications of church beliefs concerning sexuality?

AUGUSTINE OF HIPPO

A theologian arose who took on these issues in ways that determined church doctrine from his time to the present. Augustine was born in CE 354 in a town in what is now Algeria. His mother, Monica, was a devout Christian and his father, Patrick, was pagan until shortly before his death. Monica had hopes for her son and had him signed with the cross and entered as a catechumen at his birth. (Infant baptism was still rare at the time).

Augustine was brilliant and well educated. When his father died in CE 370, he had to work to support the family. He taught and was promoted to professorships in rhetoric in Carthage. According to his later writings, he was converted to Christianity in 386. He later wrote in his *Confessions* of his early life. For many years, he had a relationship with a woman who was not his wife, conceiving a son who was born in 372. He was for a time a part of the sect of Manichees discussed above. Manichaeism was a popular cult that spread as far as China and was an important movement in the West as well. In 384, Augustine moved to Milan. There, he converted to Neoplatonism, a new interpretation of the philosophy of Plato, mediated by Plotinus, a contemporary of Origen in Alexandria. Many Christians were able to incorporate their beliefs into a Neoplatonist framework.[13]

While influenced by Neoplatonism, Augustine offered his own insights into Christianity, including distinct views on the nature of sexuality. The platonic emphasis influenced him to lead a celibate life from then on. In 387 he and his son were baptized. After his mother's death, he returned to Africa and became a part of an ascetic community that later relocated to Hippo. In 395 he was consecrated a bishop. Because of his church leadership role, he began to write more concerning the Bible, especially Paul's letters. Augustine was a complex person whose brilliance led him to become a strategic contributor to theological doctrine arising from biblical understanding.[14]

In his book, *The City of God*, Augustine deals with the relationship of church and state, prompted by the diminishing power of Rome. While he did not disparage the need for the order that government may bring, he believed the need for government existed because of our fallen nature.

A most significant feature of *The City of God* was Augustine's teaching about human nature and its destiny. This feature had ongoing implications for the Bible and human sexuality, the question of evil, and the pervasive nature of human sin. Augustine became involved in theological conflict with a British monk named Pelagius. These were not the first to debate the understanding of the "fall" from grace beginning with the Garden of Eden, but theirs had implications that we continue to deal with in contemporary church life.

Pelagius asserted that human nature has within itself the power to resist sin—to choose the right path. He denied that evil existed in a newborn child. Referring to John 3, he acknowledged that although newborns need baptism and the redemption of Christ, a merciful and just God would not send a baby to hell.[15] Diarmaid MacCulloch includes a quotation by Pelagius that asserts, "That we are able to see with our eyes is no power of ours; but it is in our power that we make good or bad use of our eyes . . . the fact that we have the power of accomplishing every good thing by action, speech and thought comes from him who has endowed us with this possibility, and also assists it."[16]

Augustine asserted that the whole human race fell in Adam. I remember in history class learning the recitation of Puritan children in Massachusetts, "As in Adam's fall, we sinned all." Augustine further explained the fall as hereditary, as he explained it, the transmission of hereditary sinfulness is bound up with the reproductive process. Arguing against the Origenists (Origen, the theologian), he urged that the soul came into existence simultaneously with the body and was inseparable from it, the power of God working mysteriously on the human sperm to change it into a precious living being."[17]

Agreeing with the general belief that virginity is a higher state than marriage, Augustine was convinced that the sexual impulse can never be free of some element of lust and sexual desire.

Augustine is only one theologian among several who believed celibacy to be a higher virtue than relationships, including sexual intimacy. This viewpoint continued through the centuries, carried in part by the monastic movement, which often encouraged asceticism that included abstinence. Jerome, a church leader in Rome in the fourth century, "aroused anger by a hostility to sex and even marriage which far exceeded even the general early Christian prudishness about sexuality."[18]

We remember Paul suggesting that celibacy is a good idea, but his reasons were not that sex was ultimately sinful or that the desire for a sexual relationship was inherently wrong (1 Corinthians 7:7). He wanted new Christians to concentrate on Christ and the mission to share Christ with others. Some church leaders may have interpreted Paul in ways that he had never intended. Nevertheless, those with priestly or monastic vocations took on the vow of celibacy, a practice that continues into the present in the Roman Catholic tradition.

Augustine's teachings become controversial in the search for a Christian understanding of human sexuality because he interprets original sin as inevitable and connected to the very nature of humanity. Adam chose to sin. "His only weakness was his creatureliness which meant he was changeable by nature and so liable to turn away from the transcendent good."[19] Augustine also believed "that the taint was propagated from parent to child by the physical act of generation, or rather as the carnal excitement that accompanied it, and was present, he noticed, in the sexual intercourse even of baptized persons."[20]

Augustine, like all interpreters of God's message through Scripture, is complex in his influence on Christianity. He offered inspirational insights that continue to shape Christianity today. He reminded us that Jesus said to Pilate, "My kingdom is not from this world" (John 18:36a). We cannot finally depend on the systems or rulers of this world for what is ultimately eternal with God. He also argued for our complete dependence on God's grace. We cannot redeem ourselves or perfect ourselves in God's love. At the same time, he and those who followed him set in motion beliefs that have continued to equate sex with sin and shame concerning our bodies and our God-created sexuality.

Much in culture today mirrors Augustine's belief that there is something wrong in the very nature of sexuality. Karen A. McClintock defines shame as the need to "hide or cover up."[21] Augustine's teachings fit earlier concepts of ritual impurity and patriarchal leadership, increasingly led by celibate male clerics who became ever more the authorities for interpretation of the Bible in the life of the church.

There are many theologians and other writers who continued the development of doctrine and moral laws for the church but all cannot be discussed here. Some understood God's creation of wholeness of humanity to be good; reflecting unity of body, mind, and spirit as expressed in Genesis 1 and 2. Others continued after Augustine to follow his teachings as the correct interpretation of Scripture. We are aware of the understanding of the sexual act as intended only for procreation that became the norm in the Roman Catholic Church.

THOMAS AQUINAS

Thomas Aquinas is another enormously influential philosophical theologian. The system of thought developed by Aquinas in the thirteenth century represents a defining moment in medieval thought.[22] While Augustine was influenced by the Greek philosopher Plato in his early years, Aquinas was influenced by Plato's pupil, Aristotle. "It was in the process of approaching faith through reasoned arguments that Aquinas found Aristotle so useful, particularly Aristotle's newly translated works on metaphysics."[23] For Aquinas, all truth came together in God, but the natural world also existed in cause, effect, and change. This view takes more seriously God's fullness in creation over any vestige of Gnostic dualism with its focus on the good spiritual creation and the lesser material world.

Aquinas wrote extensively on many issues, including sexual morality. Among his writings were the *Summa Theologaie* and the *Summa Contra Gentiles*. In the *Summa Theologaie* he asks and answers questions, in one section concerning the nature of sex. One question reads, "Whether or not venereal act can be without sin." One answer is as follows: "It would seem that no venereal act can be without sin. For nothing but sin would seem to hinder virtue. Now every venereal act is a great hindrance to virtue. For Augustine says, (Soliloquy 110) 'Consider that nothing so casts down the manly mind from its height as the fondling of a woman, and those bodily contacts.' Therefore no venereal act is without sin."[24]

In the *Summa Theologaie*, Aquinas seems to rate various sexual acts as less or more serious sins. He is gentler concerning sex that doesn't hurt another person or another man's wife. Such acts are less serious in the Hebrew Scriptures as well. Again, the wife is the property of a man and the sin is against the woman's husband or her father. More serious sins include adultery and incest as described as violations of holiness in Leviticus 18–20, laws concerning rape and adultery in Deuteronomy 22:24–27, and the virginity of a woman entering into marriage in Deuteronomy 22:13–21. The *Summa* even adds a note on the sin of bestiality, or sex with animals, as declared unclean and a perversion in Leviticus 18:23.

Despite differences in theological methodology, Augustine and Aquinas seem to be similarly negative in their interpretations of sex. It is quite possible that the work of Thomas Aquinas helped the church to progress in the debate over science and religion, and in the use of reason as integral to foundational faith formation. However, in the area of biblical insight into human sexuality, it is difficult to see much change in the understanding of sexuality as a God-given gift, emphasized in the Genesis creation stories, a source of joy, only becoming harmful through willful action to possess, oppress, or hurt another human person. Is every carnal act a sin?

When the Protestant Reformation occurred several hundred years after Aquinas, the attitude toward biblical interpretation created new possibilities. Ironically, it was Martin Luther's devotion to Augustine that led him to reinterpret Scripture with the emphasis once again on the necessity of grace alone.[25] With the advent of the printing press, Bibles became available to people who could read. "*Sola scriptura*" became a key component of the Reformation. As translated from the Latin, the "*sola*" means "alone," "ground," "base." It basically meant that the Bible alone was the authority for the faith and practice of Christianity.

This premise came into conflict with some of the doctrines and practices of the Roman Catholic Church. There was less attention to some of the doctrines and practices of the Orthodox communions that had split with Rome around the year CE 1000. They also refuted doctrines that had deemed Mary sinless, a perpetual virgin, and later of her bodily assumption into heaven at her death. These doctrines of Mary had evolved over the centuries. Diarmaid MacCulloch writes of English Benedictine abbots, who in 1120 deemed her "the Mother of God, who must also have been conceived without the normal human correlation of concupiscence (lust); because her conception was immaculate, unspotted by sin, so was her flesh."[26]

Many of these doctrines have continued into the present time to influence church teachings on human sexuality. Most of these doctrines came through male theologians.

There were great women, lay and monastic, writers and spiritual leaders, in the church over the centuries, including Teresa of Avila, Julian of Norwich, and Hildegard of Bingen. They wrote on a range of topics including cosmology and medicine.[27] Most of them were celibate monastics. It seemed that women, like male monastics, did not challenge the sexual mores of the church. They concentrated on their devotion to God, prayer, ministry, and writing. Many of these women became nuns with celibacy as one of the monastic vows. Jeanne Guyon, born in 1647, was married and became a contemplative, writing spiritual books, and offering spiritual direction.[28] The witness of these women and others is of increasing influence today in the life of faith and in attitudes toward women. For some in the faith, sexual stereotypes continue.

ARMINIUS AND REFORMATION THEOLOGY

Jacobus Arminius (1560–1609) was a Dutch reformer who taught theology at the University of Leiden. During his life, he took issue with the teachings of John Calvin, especially the emphasis on unconditional election and irresistible grace. The Synod of Dort (1618–1619) condemned Arminian theology with its belief in "free-will, salvation for all and resistible grace," but it continued to be influential, finding perhaps its strongest proponent in John Wesley.[29]

Most who are of the Methodist family have heard of Wesley's confidence in "prevenient grace." It can be defined as divine grace that precedes human decision. It exists without reference to what we may have done or who we are as created beings. Prevenient grace would argue against a doctrine of the fall being passed down in the act of procreation. This grace allows us to choose salvation and to live in the confidence of grace.

CONTEMPORARY INTERPRETATIONS OF SCRIPTURE

We all bring to discernment of Scripture our whole being and all the aspects of our formation. We are persons of a certain culture at a specific time in history. We are of certain ethnic groups living in a geographic location. We are taught by parents, schools, and church leaders, and are subject to secular influences of our context. A political situation in our historical community may make a difference as to how we view Scripture. It was always like this. This chapter has discussed the theology and philosophy that shaped the beliefs and dogmas of various times, influencing what was taught regarding sexuality.

Likewise, in contemporary times we have seen a proliferation of theological thinking based on particular situations in history and culture. African Americans have reinterpreted the witness of Jesus Christ who loved all persons in his time (Samaritans, Gentiles) to emphasize the equal worth of all individuals, and have disputed interpretations of Scripture that denigrate people of color.

One damaging interpretation of race has come from the story of Ham, one of the sons of Noah. Ham may be related to the Egyptian word *kem*, meaning "Black Land." Ham thus became associated with blackness.

There are disputes about the curse falling on Canaan, rather than his father, Ham. Nevertheless, the story and Ham's being black have been used by some in the past to justify slavery and the racist view of black persons as inferior.[30]

Female authors now write extensively about theology and faith. Many seek to help everyone to understand the denigration of women throughout the centuries, in both Judaism and Christianity. Some of the books cited in this study bear their names. The work of these authors has helped women to know themselves as equal in worth to men and has contributed greatly to female leadership in the church. Many of their insights are new to persons of faith.

Parallel understandings have brought about similar changes in Western society outside the church as well. In recent years our Latin American brothers and sisters have emerged in the context of decades of poverty and oppression to offer what we call liberation theology. This has meant a new look at the witness of Jesus, interpretation of Scripture, and a call for justice for the poor and marginalized in the church and the world. Phillip Berryman says of liberation theology, "In fact, liberation theology is an interpretation of Christian faith out of the experience of the poor. It is an attempt to read the Bible and key Christian doctrines with the eyes of the poor."[31]

Berryman goes on to cite women in the liberation movement (Beatriz Couch, Julia Esquivel, Elsa Tamez), who remind us that women are twice exploited if they are of ethnic or cultural minorities. Sexual exploitation is a facet in the oppression of poor women.[32] To some traditional church leaders, these theologies seem subversive to generations of the understanding of church and Bible. What we need to understand is that traditional biblical teachings also arise from interpretation, most often by male clerics who were products of their time in history and cultural setting. These contemporary biblical scholars challenge us with new ways to reflect on Scripture and the witness of the Christian faith. The development of new understandings of Scripture has continued from the first century to the present.

I teach part-time at a small liberal arts college in Michigan. When the students introduce themselves to the class, I ask them to say something about the influences surrounding them as they were growing up. These influences come from family life and from events in the wider world. Each one in recent years remembers where they were on September 11, 2001. People from other parts of the world respond with events that impacted them in their countries and cultures just as significantly as September 11 did in the United States. Influences in personal experience and in the culture around us will always play a significant role in our interpretation of reality and faith.

As this chapter comes to an end, we conclude that while the church continued to develop with the primacy of Scripture in its formation, the interpretation of that Scripture was often subject to the influence of an individual leader. At other times, historical developments changed ideas. The millennia after Christ saw enormous developments through the fall of Rome, the medieval period, the Enlightenment, the Reformation, the expansion of Western domination, the Industrial Revolution, the growth of urban life, world wars, and our current time. Biblical interpretation was influenced by all of these.

How do we perceive Scripture today? How do we discern the sacred meaning of a passage or a book of the Bible? Why do we at times disagree with other Christians in their interpretations of Scripture? What for each of us is a biblical ethic that most reflects Jesus Christ as we better understand human sexuality? How will we develop a sexual ethic for ourselves and our church as we seek guidance from the witness of those who have sought to discern the will of God and who have given us their insights through their interpretations of Scriptures? We will need to reflect on the ways in which God leads each of us and the community of the church in faithfully interpreting the Bible in our own time. Chapter 5 continues the discussion of faithful biblical interpretation and how we apply it to our lives of spirit and action for Christ.

Endnotes

1. Isaac Klmi, "Lydia, Lydians," in *The New Interpreter's Dictionary*, 3:736.
2. J. N. D. Kelly, *Early Christian Doctrines* (San Francisco: Harper, 1978), 23.
3. Ibid., 24.
4. Bruce M. Metzger and Michael D. Coogan, *The Oxford Guide to the Bible*, 256.
5. Henry Chadwick, *The Early Church* (London: Penguin Books, 1993), 39.

6. Ibid., 40.

7. J. N. D. Kelly, *Early Christian Doctrines* (San Francisco: Harper, 1978), 26–27.

8. Diarmaid MacCulloch, *Christianity: The First Three Thousand Years* (London: Penguin Books, 2011), 156.

9. Elaine Pagels, *The Gnostic Gospels* (New York: Random House, Vintage Books, 1981), 77–78.

10. Ibid., 170.

11. Riane Eisler, *Chalice and Blade*, 130.

12. Diarmaid MacCulloch, *Christianity: The First Three Thousand Years*, 212.

13. Ibid., 170.

14. Henry Chadwick, *The Early Church*, 216–219.

15. Ibid., 228.

16. Diarmaid MacCulloch, *Christianity: The First Three Thousand Years*, 306, (quoting J. Stevenson, ed. W.H.C. Frend, *Creeds, Councils and Controversies,* 1989, 232–3).

17. J.N.D. Kelly, *Early Christian Doctrines*, 345.

18. Diarmaid MacCulloch, *Christianity: The First Three Thousand Years*, 314.

19. J.N.D. Kelly, *Early Christian Doctrines*, 362.

20. Ibid., 363.

21. Karen R. McClintock, *Sexual Shame: An Urgent Call to Healing* (Minneapolis: Fortress Press, 2001), 21.

22. Diarmaid MacCulloch, *Christianity: The First Three Thousand Years*, 412.

23. Ibid., 413.

24. Paul Halsall Mar "Medieval Sourcebook: Aquinas on *Unnatural* Sex," from Internet Medieval Source Book, Fordham University, Summa Theologiae ll–ll, question 153.2, accessed November 11, 2014, http://legacy.fordham.edu/halsall/source/aquinas-homo.asp.

25. Diarmaid MacCulloch, *Christianity: The First Three Thousand Years*, 606.

26. Ibid., 394.

27. Diarmaid MacCulloch, *Christianity: The First Three Thousand Years*, 420.

28. Jeanne Guyon, *Selected Writings, Classics of Western Spirituality*, Introduction I. Brief Biography (Mahwah, NJ: Paulist Press, 2011), 27–28.

29. The Wesley Center Online, homepage, accessed December 5, 2014, http://wesley.nnu.edu.

30. *The New Interpreter's Dictionary of the Bible*, 2:724.

31. Phillip Berryman, *Liberation Theology: Essential Facts About the Revolutionary Movement in Latin America and Beyond* (New York: Pantheon Books, 1987), 4.

32. Ibid., 172.

✺ ✺ ✺ CHAPTER 5

Take Authority

When I was ordained as an elder of The United Methodist Church, I put my hand on the Bible and was told to "take authority as an elder in the church to preach the Word of God and to administer the Holy Sacraments."[1] I have attempted to faithfully follow that admonition. We, as United Methodists, also believe that every person of faith who seeks to know more of Christ and God's desire for humanity should take upon herself or himself authority regarding the discernment of God's Word for God's people.

One evening years ago, we were hard at work on a lesson in our Disciple Bible Study materials. As is often the case in a Bible study group, smaller groups were discussing Bible passages, seeking to plumb the depths of their meaning. The group came back together and discernment was shared. One woman seemed a bit puzzled at the process. She finally looked around the room and commented, "I understand it now. We are expected to offer our individual interpretations to the discussion, even if they are not the same as someone else's view." She was right. We have received both the gift and the responsibility to prayerfully read, study, and discern the meaning of Scripture for our lives and for the church.

Thus far in this study, we have encountered widely divergent views of the meaning of selected biblical passages. We read Genesis 1 and perceived a creative, powerful God who calls all creation into being and calls it good. This includes the man and woman made in God's image; beings who can think and choose; sexual beings made for relationships of love and intimacy. Different interpretations of the Bible over the years have both affirmed sexuality as a part of God's gracious creation and regarded sexuality as the very nature of original sin. Sexuality was enthusiastically embraced in the Song of Songs and yet regulated by laws which determined that sex and procreation must be fulfilled in ways that made mother and wife the property of father and husband.

Some Gnostics among the early Christians believed that only the spiritual was important in relationship to God; the material world being either evil or of no importance. That view was forcefully countered by a great leader of the church in the late second century, Irenaeus. He interpreted the Word to affirm the whole created nature of humanity, "For the glory of God is the human person fully alive; and life consists in beholding God. For if the vision of God, which is made by means of the creation, gives life to all living on earth, much more does that revelation of the Father which comes through the Word, give life to those who see God."[2]

Differing interpretations of Scripture have always existed. There are those who believe that the Scripture can be taken literally, word for word as written. Many faithful people over the centuries and even today believe this. Yet we must ask ourselves, "Whose literal interpretation are we to believe?"

This becomes a question of authority. In the Jewish-Christian tradition, there have been teachers and prophets who were the respected interpreters of Scripture. Remember the young Jesus sitting at the feet of the rabbis, teachers in the temple. Jesus said later in the Sermon on the Mount, "Do not think I have come to abolish the law or the prophets; I have come not to abolish but to fulfill" (Matthew 5:17). He continues the sermon by interpreting the deeper meaning of the commandments. Anger with a brother or sister can be under the same judgment as murder (Matthew 5:21–26). Lust can be judged as adultery (Matthew 5:27–30).

Jesus is interpreting Scripture for the people who have come to hear him. He changes the interpretation of an eye for an eye and a tooth for a tooth to turning the other cheek, offering one's coat and also one's cloak, and going with someone a second mile (Matthew 5:38–42). He gives new insight to the old saying, "You have heard that it was said, 'You shall love your neighbor and hate your enemy.' But I say to you, love your enemies and pray for those who persecute you" (Matthew 5:43-44). Followers of Jesus understood that he brought new insights to the Scriptures. They learned lessons of life, love, and faith. The early church was also at first open to new understandings of Scripture as Gentile and Jewish believers came together in Christ.

Later we learned that authority came to rest with church leaders who were expected to teach the Word to the congregations. More and more, the authority passed to the clergy who interpreted the meaning of Scripture for the laity. These interpretations became the rules for living in daily life and for the functioning of the church. In Western Christianity, the office of the Roman Catholic pope became the chief authority, believed to be the primary revelation of God for the church. Interpretation of Scripture came from a top-down process. Bibles were not available to the common people.

The Reformation and the invention of the printing press made the Bible accessible to those who could read, but the tradition of teaching coming from the clergy and other biblical scholars continued in many places. Even today, we can attend worship or watch television and see a preacher interpret a passage of Scripture, verse by verse, telling the congregation what it means. Truth for many of us comes from the Holy Spirit speaking through many persons, not a single leader or authority.

The authority and interpretation of Scripture allows and encourages a process involving more than one way of seeking biblical truth. Each of us needs to examine the question of authority as we seek to understand God's Word to us and to the community. What are the components of faithful interpretation that can help us discern God's Word? How can we learn more about the Bible and its message for the time in which we live?

The Book of Discipline of The United Methodist Church 2012 provides guidelines for United Methodists, encouraging all persons in the denomination to engage the Scriptures. Scripture is discussed under the heading "Our Theological Task." These paragraphs are a part of that statement:

"As we open our minds and hearts to the Word of God through the words of human beings inspired by the Holy Spirit, faith is born and nourished, our understanding is deepened, and the possibilities for transforming the world become apparent to us."

"While we acknowledge the primacy of Scripture in theological reflection, our attempts to grasp its meaning always involve tradition, experience, and reason. Like Scripture, these may become creative vehicles of the Holy Spirit as they function within the church. They quicken our faith, open our eyes to the wonder of God's love, and clarify our understanding."

"Through this faithful reading of Scripture, we may come to know the truth of the biblical message in its bearing on our own lives and the life of the world. Thus, the Bible serves both as a source of our faith and as the basic criterion by which the truth and fidelity of any interpretation of faith is measured."[3]

These statements indicate that there are many ways to approach the Scriptures, seeking their truth for our individual lives of faith and for our life in the larger community of the church and the world. We begin with the expectation that God speaks to God's people through the Bible. Many of us also believe that God is present in other ways as well, but the Bible has come to us through the centuries with the understandings of those who sought to faithfully interpret God's Word.

The Scriptures contain history, theology, narrative, poetry, stories, and other forms of great literature. Yet for persons of faith, the Bible is so much more; it is the testimony of the faithful over the centuries. Did they get everything right? Did they all agree with one another? We must allow the writers of the Bible to be as human as we are. They wrote what they discerned from their own experience by opening their lives, minds, and hearts to God. We draw for our interpretation upon the long tradition of those who were inspired by the Holy Spirit and who wrote what they believed to be the truth.

We are at the same time encouraged to bring *reason* to the task. Humanity continues to explore and to learn. Science continues to discover new truth about creation and the universe. Reason aids us in new understandings of ourselves, including our sexuality. *Experience* shapes us as it has shaped our forebears in new ways. All of these affect our own experience of the Holy Spirit speaking to us and through us, sometimes with a new voice in our contemporary world.

Perhaps it is best to begin by emulating the tradition of engaging the Word with the purpose of deepening our faith. It has been my privilege over the years to attend workshops, retreats, and other experiential events that have helped me to receive more prayerfully what the Scriptures say to me and to receive the insights of others who offer their gifts. Many of these experiences spring from the spiritual lives of individuals and communities of Christians over the years.

There are those who follow the Rule of St. Benedict who, with his sister Scholastica, founded an order that followed a particular rule of life that included daily prayer and the recitation of the Psalms. Diana Butler Bass cites St. Benedict as one who discovered the Christian past in new ways in the sixth century.[4] I once had the privilege of attending a retreat at an Episcopalian Benedictine center where monks followed the Benedictine practices, and from that experience I can testify personally to the power of that rule.

St. Francis of Assisi drew upon Scripture in his founding of the Franciscan order, emphasizing poverty and the honoring of all created life. One particular passage was deeply formative: "Therefore I tell you, do not worry about your life, what you eat or what you will drink, or about your body, what you will wear. Is not life more than clothing? Look at the birds of the air; they neither sow nor reap nor gather into barns, and your heavenly Father feeds them. Are you not of more value than they?" (Matthew 6:25–26).[5]

Study of scriptural resources is essential in deepening the understanding of the meaning of Scripture. Whether this occurs in a personal or group Bible study setting, discovering more about the history, style of writing, knowledge of the authorship, and the like can add to greater understanding of Scripture. As we have noted above, the context does make a difference. What was the historical and cultural situation when a particular book was written? Most good Bible study curriculum resources available to local churches offer this sort of information. Various commentaries offer additional information. This use of study resources is particularly important for understanding the Bible and human sexuality.

As we addressed previously in this study, we ask why did the Hebrew tribes develop purity rituals and codes of law? What was the impact of the nearby cultures? What were the priorities in their understanding of God's Word to them as a people? We have all heard some teachers of Scripture apply to contemporary life admonitions that were particular to another time and context in human history. Many people discover new and great meaning in the Bible when they understand the *when, where,* and *who* of the written Word. The *why* becomes clearer and can offer insight as to what is eternal and what is ever changing.

I have received some of my greatest insights into the meaning of Scripture from other people. Yes, it is exciting to sit in the presence of a great Bible teacher and glean from that person the wisdom that comes from concentration in Bible study. Scholars, pastors, and lay teachers of Sunday school and Bible study groups can offer perspectives that can help persons deepen their walk with God's message through the Bible.

At the same time, equally profound insights and wisdom have come through those attending Bible study groups who have no special training, but who have come to the Scriptures faithfully, prayerfully, and open to what they may receive. Together groups of Christians journey in faith through Scripture as they pray, learn, discuss, and ask the deep questions of life with the expectation that the Bible may point them toward answers.

There are other ways to enhance the study of Scripture as we use our God-given imagination to plumb the depth of meaning in a story or passage. For instance, role-plays can enable us to place ourselves in the biblical story that is being read, and to feel what the biblical characters might have felt. What must it have felt like to be the woman caught in adultery, standing there expecting to be stoned to death and suddenly finding herself alone with Jesus bent over and writing on the ground? (John 8:1–11). What did the woman who touched Jesus' cloak go through during those twelve years she bled? What must she have felt in that crowd as she came to the decision to go to him and touch his garment? What is it like to be healed after all that time? What did it feel like to risk coming forward in that crowd and admit she was the one who touched him? There are many ways to make the experience of Scripture our own, to experience how God has been revealed in the past and is being revealed today. Using a phrase that appears in the *Book of Discipline*, we can say that the Bible is "enlivened in experience" when we seek to engage the Scriptures at the deepest level.

Scripture, tradition, experience, and reason are four ways of approaching faith to receive God's love in Christ and God's truth that is offered to us. Each of us is to take upon ourselves the authority to discern and interpret the message of Scripture for ourselves and for the community that calls us to learn and grow together. Scripture, tradition, experience, and reason are wonderful tools to broaden interpretation. With these tools of interpretation and the desire to grow in understanding of what God is saying to us in the twenty-first century, we need to examine the issues of human sexuality, using the Bible as a primary guide in seeking insight for ourselves and for our witness to the world. Given the differing views of sexuality among the many writers and interpreters of Scripture over the centuries, it is difficult to write a rule book for sexual conduct that takes into account that historical diversity and also speaks to the reality most of us experience today. Above all, we should seek a sexual ethic that is consistent with our understanding of God who came to us as the Christ.

Maxine Beach in the study, *The Bible: The Book that Bridges the Millennia: Part 2: Interpretation & Authority* asks some key questions: "In spite of the long history of diverse interpretations of Holy Scriptures, Christians agree that the Bible was inspired by God. But what does 'inspired' mean? The word comes from the Latin for 'breathe,' the root of the word 'spirit,' and literally means 'breathed into.' If we agree the Bible is divinely inspired, does that mean that God dictated every word? Breathed it into the minds and hearts of the writers? Gave it to them in visions? Might it mean that each writer interpreted God based on the inspiration of an experience of the divine? Do we understand that angry, vengeful, or sexist passages are also divinely inspired? Can something divinely inspired be less than perfect? Is Scripture 'holy' because it is perfect, or because it contains the faith and practices necessary for salvation?"[6] In reflecting on these questions, we might have the beginnings of a sexual ethic that is scriptural, informed by tradition and reason, and enlivened by our faith experience.

I recently was introduced to the work of Barbara Lee, who was theologically educated in the Lutheran tradition and speaks and writes concerning attitudes toward human sexuality in contemporary culture. On November 7, 2013, she gave a TED Talk at TEDx Muskegon (Michigan) where she lives and works. In the talk she explored issues of human sexuality that often puzzle us and sometimes divide us. She suggested a beginning point for developing a sexual ethic: "To relate to each other as whole human beings, we need to develop and live by a Sexual Ethic that celebrates sex while treating it with moral integrity. An ethic that begins by recognizing that people of all sexual orientations and gender identities, of all marital status and of all physical capacities, have the right to experience sex as a healthy and life giving part of their existence."[7]

This concept is amplified in the work of Bruce C. Birch in his book, *To Love As We Are Loved: The Bible and Relationships*, "Our relationship with God comes to us, in the testimony of the biblical witnesses, as a freely given gift.

We are called into relationship by the freely given grace of God. We have the possibility of meaningful interaction with others as a gift and not as a duty. We make free choices about relationships, rather than relate by instinctual pattern like other animals. Thus we were created for relationship to one another in freedom."[8]

In many discussions of biblical truth over the years a primary question has emerged, "What would Jesus do?" This is not a bad place to begin. We must look to what might be called "Christ consciousness" and ask how it illumines issues of concern. What was the consciousness or attitude of Jesus, offered to us in the biblical witness, in our life of prayer, and in our many ministries of justice and peace? What gives us the insight we need to understand the way of Jesus Christ as we witness to our faith? What are the foundation stones of Scripture that become the bedrock of our faith? The issues that confront us today are myriad. Chapter 6 will pose some of those issues and examine ways we might approach those issues through the inspiration of Scripture in the consciousness of Christ, seeking to form a sexual ethic for our time.

Endnotes

1. *The Book of Discipline of The United Methodist Church 2012*, Social Principles (Nashville: Abingdon Press, 2012), 256.

2. Diana Butler Bass, *A People's History of Christianity* (New York: HarperOne, 1989), 39.

3. *The Book of Discipline of The United Methodist Church 2012*, Social Principles, 82.

4. Butler Bass, *A People's History of Christianity*, 22.

5. Ibid., 137–138.

6. Maxine Beach, *The Bible: The Book that Bridges the Millennia, Part 2: Interpretation and Authority*, 139.

7. Barbara Lee, "Creating a Sexual Ethic" in *Sacred Sex* (Splattered Ink Press, 2013), 32–37.

8. Bruce Birch, *To Love As We Are Loved: The Bible and Relationships*, 11.

✵ ✵ ✵ CHAPTER 6

Developing a Sexual Ethic for Our Time

We are aware of conflicting views about the status of women as we consider a sexual ethic for our time, it is a sexuality that reflects biblical principles, loving relationships, family life, and other issues that affect our bodies and our health. Once again, we know that for people of faith, biblical interpretation can be at the root of the conflict. As we discussed in Chapter 5, sincere efforts to interpret Scripture faithfully can still find us not always agreeing on the meaning of a particular passage or chapter or how we are meant to live a life based on a particular scriptural rule or principle.

The work of developing a sexual ethic of both spiritual and moral value can be for us an intensive, exciting process. It requires us to look deeply into ourselves in ways that open our minds and spirits to the biblical message. We must listen carefully to others as they share their discernment regarding human sexuality. We must examine scriptural references, asking ourselves what they meant at the time they were written and what they say to us now. We must take into consideration the reality that there may be differences of interpretation among us, each person having offered their discernment in faithful dialogue.

We need to develop a sexual ethic for our time that covers individual and family sexuality, but goes on to address the desperate need for sexual justice for innocent persons who are victimized day after day. Some of these victims live closer to us than we want to believe. Young girls and young boys are taken from their homes and trafficked to places of sexual exploitation. Domestic abuse happens in rich and poor families alike. Sexual assault is an issue on college campuses. In all of our lives, sexism lurks just beneath the surface.

Some people are marginalized because of their sexual orientation. What does the Bible say to help us navigate these issues of modern-day sexuality?

GENDER ISSUES IN THE BIBLE AND CONTEMPORARY TIMES

Many of us who are Christian have a strong expectation that women will be considered equal in value to men. At the same time, there are those who would conserve traditional understandings of the roles of men and women. In Genesis 1, both are created in the image of God. We also know the attitude and practice of Jesus. He discussed theology with the woman at the well in Samaria (John 4:1–30), listened to a woman remind him that God's love included non-Jews (Matthew 15:21–28), and validated the leadership of the women who followed him in addition to the twelve men who were apostles. This reinforces the purpose of the Creator who came in Christ.

Women over the centuries have been honored as Christians. Recall the biblical accounts of Jesus revealing his resurrected presence to the women who loved him and stayed with him to the end. Later, Paul reminded the growing Christian community that in Christ all are equal (Galatians 3:28). While Paul may have been inconsistent in some of his writings, he recognized and depended on the leadership of women as well as men in establishing churches throughout the Roman world.

Other interpreters rely on a more hierarchal understanding of women and family. Ephesians 5 asserts that a husband is head of the wife, just as Christ is head of the church: "Wives must be subject to their husbands in everything." The passage goes on to say that a man must love his wife as he does his own body, just as Christ loves the church. In Ephesians 6, the author speaks of the obedience to be given by children and also by slaves, who are to obey their earthly masters with fear and trembling, doing the will of God from the heart (Ephesians 5:21–6:9). 1 Peter asks husbands to show consideration to their wives as the weaker sex (1 Peter 3:7). 1 Timothy includes duties for widows

(1 Timothy 5:3–16). This highlights the fact that differing interpretations of the Bible do indeed affect attitudes and policies toward women and men today.

Some continue to believe that a husband is head of the household. Mirabel Morgan affirmed this in her 1970s book *The Total Woman*. She stated, "The Biblical remedy for marital conflict is stated, 'You wives must submit to your husband's leadership in the same way you submit to the Lord.' God planned for woman to be under her husband's rule."[1] This continues to be the belief of many evangelical Christians at the present time. Not long ago, I attended a wedding where the bride promised to obey her husband in this manner.

On the other hand, Virginia Ramey Mollenkott in *Women, Men and the Bible*, says, "If my analysis of the Christian way of relating has been accurate—and I urge you to study the New Testament and check every reference and context for yourself—and if what Christ and the apostles teach really is mutual submissive love and concern, then we may expect that human experience shows that this is indeed the healthiest, most adult, most positive form of human relating."[2]

BODY IMAGE AND HEALTH

Psalm 139:13–14 says, "For it was you who formed my inward parts; you knit me together in my mother's womb. I praise you, for I am fearfully and wonderfully made. Wonderful are your works; that I know very well." Someone asked, "What is so fearful and wonderful about the way God made us?" S. Michael Houdmann answered the question in this way, "The context of this verse is the incredible nature of our physical bodies. The human body is the most complex and unique organism in the world, and that complexity and uniqueness speaks volumes about the mind of its Creator. Every aspect of the body, down to the tiniest microscopic cell, reveals that it is fearfully and wonderfully made."[3]

As we form a sexual ethic, we must understand our bodies as a gift from the God who created us and called us good. In the Hebrew Scriptures, the body is considered good. The purpose of many of the rituals and purity codes affecting the body were to keep the body pure. This positive view of our bodies persisted into New Testament times among the first Christians who were Jewish in practice. There is therefore precedence in Scripture for us to regard our bodies as the gift they are intended to be and to care for this precious gift throughout our lives.

The Social Principles of The United Methodist Church state under the heading "Right to Health Care" that "Health is a condition of physical, mental, social and spiritual well-being. John 10:10b says, 'I came so that they could have life—indeed, so that they could live life to the fullest.'"[4] The Social Principles go on to state that "stewardship of health is the responsibility of each person …"

Honoring our bodies as a gift from God must be part of any faithful sexual ethic. Such honoring of the body extends beyond each of us into the world, and becomes a social, cultural, and justice issue. We live in an age when attitudes and practices of sexuality exhibit themselves on a lengthy continuum. Men as well as women are affected by these attitudes and practices. Many boys and girls are taught by family and community the significance of their bodies. Some of the teachings can be healthy and some perpetuate harmful stereotypes of both sexes. Men are supposed to be strong and able to be physically aggressive, taking charge of their families. Some women, on the other hand, come to see themselves as sexual objects to be coveted for their overt sexual attributes. We see this frequently in advertising that shows the female physical body, deemed beautiful because of large breasts, slim legs, and sensuous buttocks. The purpose of life for many women exists in their relationship with and approval of men. This affects the way women dress, what freedom or lack thereof they are allowed, their place at home or in a workplace and in the lives of their children.[5] Those who have succumbed to the view of having the perfect body as a way of being accepted are part of what drives diet fads and other programs to change their bodies. The lure of this is that someone will love us if we are beautiful on the outside. To grow older is anathema, but even that can supposedly be halted with the right products to defy the wrinkles and gray hair. Men often share the same fear of aging and look to diets and body building in order to stay attractive.

Both ends of the female continuum suggest a sense of sexual shame. One end of a female continuum is the pure virgin woman who is ashamed of sexual desire. The other end is the woman who expresses her sexual desire in her revealing clothing and promiscuous behavior. In *Sexual Shame*, Karen A. McClintock writes, "Family therapists Marilyn Mason and Merle Fossum define shame as 'an inner sense of being completely diminished or insufficient as a person.'. . . A pervasive sense of shame is the ongoing premise that one is fundamentally bad, inadequate, defective, unworthy, or not fully valid as a human being."[6] Unfortunately, some of the sexual shame may come from biblical interpretations that fail to remind people how loved and blessed they are. Passages in 1 Peter and some of the teachings of Augustine, discussed above, are examples. McClintock's book urges us in the church to become more open to discussion of shame, body issues, and stereotypes of sexuality. The church is too often silent on these issues.

McClintock also makes a helpful distinction between shame and guilt, a distinction that needs to be part of the discussion in our churches since ideas of shame and guilt continue to affect culture and faith. McClintock explains:

> Confusion frequently arises about the difference between guilt and shame. They are not the same. Guilt is the conscience telling us that we have done something wrong. It serves as a protection for us, as a warning sign that we have violated our own values. With guilt we have injured ourselves by a behavior that is unacceptable. The action is judged wrong (either internally or externally) and must be amended. If we go through a process of confession, forgiveness, and restoration, the guilt is relieved. With shame, actions are not the whole story. Our very beings are at fault. It isn't simply that I have hurt my brother, but that I am not worthy of my brother's forgiveness. When the prodigal son returned to his father's house, the father had forgiven him for his actions.

The young man said to him "I am no longer worthy to be called your son, treat me like one of your hired servants" (Luke 15:19). The father's treatment of him as royalty was the cure for his shame. He told the boy that no matter what his actions had been—the throwing away of the inheritance, the "dissolute living" (Luke 19:13; a sexual matter?)—he needn't hang his head in shame. He was accepted, restored and honored.[7]

For those who are United Methodist, issues of human sexuality are included in the statements made in the Social Principles, paragraph 162, section III The Social Community, paragraph F, Rights of Women—We affirm women and men to be equal in every aspect of common life. "We therefore urge that every effort be made to eliminate sex-role stereotypes in activity and portrayal of family life and in all aspects of voluntary and compensatory participation in the church and society."[8] Such statements seek to reflect the Word in a changing world, believing that God is revealed ever new among the people who desire to know God more fully through the Holy Spirit working in their lives and in the community.

RELATIONSHIPS AND INTIMACY

A sexual ethic begins with receiving the gift of our wondrously made bodies and accepting responsibility for decisions of physical and spiritual health and welfare for all persons. It extends into the church and world. This ethic must share the blessing of God with others, especially teaching children that their bodies are precious gifts and that there is no shame with regard to their sexuality. In the world, we need an ethic that includes ministries of justice for victims of violence and poverty.

For Christians, a sexual ethic must also be centered in Christ as we encounter him in Scripture. Jesus the Christ is the ground of our being as we seek to open ourselves to God through the Holy Spirit. We may have differing interpretations of some of the things Jesus said, but the New Testament seems very clear that Jesus put relationships first.

At times even those who were the closest to Jesus failed to understand his complete ministry. He blessed children when the disciples would have sent them away (Matthew 19:13–15). He healed people who were blind, lame, and mentally ill. Some of them were Gentiles. He was there for all: women, men, and children. He taught his disciples that we all need to become as humble as children who know nothing more than to be true to themselves (Matthew 18:1–5). This teaching encourages us to accept the good gift of our sexuality.

We can speak eloquently, write books of theology, develop rules and dogmas to define the church, but if we fail to live in loving relationships, we have not lived as if Christ lived in us. How many times have we heard the words of 1 Corinthians 13, "If I speak with the tongues of mortals and of angels, but do not have love, I am a noisy gong or a clanging cymbal. And if I have prophetic powers, and understand all mysteries and all knowledge, and if I have all faith so as to remove mountains, but do not have love, I am nothing. If I give away all my possessions, and if I hand over my body so that I may boast, but do not have love, I gain nothing"? (1 Corinthians 13:1–3). In the end, Christian faith is about loving relationships with those near to–us, with all persons, and with all of creation.

Bruce Birch writes, "Thus, to reflect God's righteousness in our relationships to one another is not just a matter of learning the right things to do or rules about when to do them. Righteousness has to do with the quality of our relationships—the identity we carry with us into relationship and the new identity that becomes ours in relationship."[9]

Another way to speak of relationship is to use the language of covenant. The Bible is full of covenants: covenants with Noah, Abraham, Moses, and David. Such covenants were promises made between God and the people. The two parties in the covenants were not equal in nature, as God is the Holy One, the Creator. God expected the people to honor and be obedient to the covenant. God did not break promises, but sometimes the people did.

In New Testament times, Christians came to understand that they were part of a new covenant made through the life, death, and resurrection of Christ. Paul wrote, "Such is the confidence we have in Christ toward God, not that we are competent of ourselves to claim anything as coming from us; our competence is from God who has made us to be ministers of a new covenant, not of letter but of spirit; for the letter kills, but the Spirit gives life" (2 Corinthians 3:4–6). The concept of covenant provides hope for life in the community of the church and beyond. The notion of covenant emphasizes the relational and communal aspect of life, expressed in human relationships and in humanity's relationship with the rest of creation.

There is a close connection between covenant and "steadfast love." "Forever I will keep my steadfast love for him, and my covenant will stand firm" (Psalm 89:28). Here the psalmist understands a covenant with God to be one of steadfast, eternal love. The notion of relationship as grounded in covenant and commitment has come to be a part of a Christian understanding of sexuality and the intimacy shared by two persons, families, and communities.

As a pastor, I have often used the language of covenantal commitment in marriage preparation. The statement on marriage in the Social Principles begins, "We affirm the sanctity of the marriage covenant that is expressed in love, mutual support, personal commitment and shared fidelity" and goes on to state that marriage is between a man and a woman.[10]

CHANGING VIEWS OF MARRIAGE

Judgment involving sexuality often falls more on women than on men. Not too many years ago the guilt of pregnancy before marriage fell most heavily on the woman. If there was no marriage, she was often looked down upon. Many of us as women and girls grew up in a culture that assumed that it was up to the woman to be the disciplined one in heterosexual relationships. Many were taught that boys and men have more sexual libido and can't discipline themselves. If a girl gave in to sex she was often labeled "fast" or "loose." This did not apply to the boys.

In the 1960s and 1970s, times changed. Gender and racial equality brought about new opportunities for women and minorities. At the same time what some called the "sexual revolution" changed sexual expectations. More people seemed to opt for living together before marriage. Many people of faith who continued to seek guidance from the Scriptures began to ask new questions. Changes in gender attitudes influenced sexuality as well as other aspects of life for women. There was more affirmation of the mutual enjoyment of sexual intimacy. Women were encouraged to better understand their bodies and their need for sexual pleasure. Marriage for many women and men became more of an equal partnership, each sharing their gifts for building up the other.

While Paul has been maligned for his statements about women, he states in 1 Corinthians 7, "The husband should give his wife her conjugal rights, and likewise the wife to her husband. For the wife does not have authority over her body, but the husband does; likewise the husband does not have authority over his body, but the wife does. Do not deprive one another except perhaps by agreement for a set time, to devote yourselves to prayer, and then come together again, so that Satan does not tempt you because of your lack of self-control" (1 Corinthians 7:3–5). The implication here is mutuality in a relationship of love.

At present, there are many couples that make the decision to become intimate before marriage. People are waiting longer to marry, and some deny the need for marriage at all. What will determine a sexual ethic or covenant for such couples? How can the church minister to them? At the same time faithful same-sex couples seek the blessing of marriage for their covenant. How do we in the church respond to their desire to affirm their covenant?

It is clear in Scripture and in Christian tradition that marriage is intended to be a lifelong commitment. However, when a relationship is irreparably broken or abusive, divorce may be better than continuing in the marriage. The New Testament in numerous places, following the example of Jesus, urges us not to judge each other, but to love one another and to forgive.

Jesus, in John 4, discussed above, shared in deep conversation with the Samaritan woman and accepted her as a worthy person. Many have come to believe the love of Christ does not hold persons in a covenant that is broken beyond healing. Few of us today would ask a woman or a man to stay in a marriage when domestic abuse is present and the abuser refuses to seek treatment. Spousal abuse can be both physical and spiritual. The Social Principles state, "When a married couple is estranged beyond reconciliation, even after thoughtful consideration and counsel, divorce is a regrettable alternative in the midst of brokenness."[11] Here the sense of biblical authority comes from an overriding belief that God desires a full life for every person. Most of us know wonderful people who have come to understand that their marriage is no longer healthy for them. Many have spent time with marriage counselors before the decision to divorce is finalized. The decision can be very painful when young children are involved. The couple may decide that their continuing estrangement may be even more difficult for the children.

There are other reasons that can separate couples; but the hope is that those who revere formation through Scripture do seek counsel. When this is impossible, the church should respect the decision and follow the admonition of Scripture not to judge, but to support and love. We need to remind ourselves often that Jesus said, "Do not judge, so that you may not be judged. For with the judgment you make, you will be judged, and the measure you give will be the measure you get" (Matthew 7:1–2). I was a part of a church community that found ways to support husband and wife and their children through a time of divorce. It was a significant ministry, and a vital one for the family and for the church.

HOMOSEXUALITY

Today many of us ask if the same commitment, the same covenant, needs to be understood in expanding ways. The Social Principles currently affirm sexual relations in monogamous, heterosexual marriage. The Social Principles do not condone the practice of homosexuality, considering it "incompatible with Christian teaching."[12] Many people of faith, United Methodist and others, are comfortable with these statements. But there are people who are equally faithful who experience the presence of the sacred in relationships that are not considered acceptable in the statements above.

We need to ponder the Scriptures as to what they say and don't say about homosexuality. We should prayerfully ponder our own experience. Most Christians today know persons who are LGBTQ (lesbian, gay, bisexual, transgendered, questioning, or queer). Some of them are our children, grand-children, siblings, and friends. Some of them are persons of faith who are living out their commitment to Christ in the life of the church.

With regard to the church, Eugene F. Rogers, Jr., in *Sexuality and the Christian Body* notes that the biblical truth of the New Testament is the grace offered to all through baptism. "Neither traditionalists nor revisionists may read their fellow Christians out of the community of baptism."[13] The weight of the centuries has condemned homosexual relationships. But there are those who have taken a new look at the Scriptures concerning homosexuality and a new look at many of our sisters and brothers in Christ of LGBTQ orientation. We need to study more, pray more, and love more as we seek clarity on this issue.

Theologian Walter Wink wrote a pamphlet entitled *Homosexuality and the Bible* that can be summed up by saying that the Scriptures included in the pamphlet must be discussed in the context in which they were written. One of his examples relates to Leviticus 20:13, "You shall not lie with a male as with a woman; it is an abomination." The author gives reasons for such a state-ment. "It was assumed that the woman provided only the incubating space."[14] This meant that the prevailing belief was that the male semen contained all of the new life and the woman was needed only as a host to grow and birth that new life. In ancient Israel any sexual act that prohibited the birth of children was forbidden, although enjoyment of sex during pregnancy or after menopause was permitted.

A reference is made in Romans 1:26 regarding persons both male and female giving in to lust and degrading their bodies with unnatural intercourse. (Female homosexual acts are not otherwise mentioned in the Hebrew Scriptures.) Wink points out that none of the negative references about homosexuality refer directly to committed relationships between same-sex partners. Such committed relationships were largely unknown in the ancient world, or unacknowledged for fear of violence. Wink asks the reader to look with new eyes at the Scriptures in the light of new experience and he concludes by saying, "We in the church need to get our priorities straight. We have not reached a consensus about who is right on the issue of homosexuality. But what is clear, utterly clear is that we are commanded to love each other. Love not just our gay sisters and brothers, who are often sitting beside us, unacknowledged in church, but all of us who are involved in this debate."[15]

A more recent resource is *What the Bible Really Says about Homosexuality* by Daniel Helminiak, a Roman Catholic priest who has ministered to the Roman Catholics through Dignity, a support group for the Catholic gay community. The dedication of his book says, "To lesbian women and gay men who believe in a good God and reverence the Bible and who want to be able to believe in themselves."[16] He includes a verse from Romans, "Let us therefore no longer pass judgment on one another, but resolve instead never to put a stumbling block or hindrance in the way of another. I know and am persuaded in the Lord Jesus that nothing is unclean in itself; but it is unclean for anyone who thinks it is unclean" (Romans 14:13–14).

Helminiak goes on to discuss the Scriptures linked to attitudes concerning homosexuality. He includes the sin of Sodom, which can be interpreted as a failure of hospitality (Genesis 19:1–11, Ezekiel 16:49). The men of Sodom sought to humiliate the visitors by sodomizing them (through anal intercourse). To humiliate men was to make them "effeminate." This was worse than having actual male-to-male sex. But the view that the sin of Sodom was primarily about homosexuality persisted for centuries.

Helminiak cites several historical Christian leaders as speaking against bodily desire for persons of the same gender. "St. Augustine wrote, the body of a man is superior to that of a woman as the soul is to the body."[17] Is there a vestige of that in our own culture when a boy teases another boy by saying, "You run like a girl"? Helminiak's ultimate conclusion is that the Bible does not prioritize a view of same-sex relationships as negative per se.

REPRODUCTIVE HEALTH

An adequate sexual ethic for our time must also consider such issues as reproductive health and family planning that may include contraception and at times termination of a pregnancy. A key portion of the health issue for women is related to deciding when and if to have a child. This decision most often includes the husband or partner. I am aware as a result of years of marriage consultation with couples that the input of both persons in the covenant as to whether to have children, when to have them, and how many, is invaluable.

There are now new configurations of persons who desire a child or children as a part of their lives. More and more single women, or, at times, men, are choosing to raise a child. There are same-sex couples that seek to love and raise children.

Family planning includes the prevention of pregnancy until the persons are ready to receive a new life into their relationship. They need to be ready to sacrifice some of themselves to become good and faithful parents, loving their children unconditionally. There are also those committed couples that decide not to have children. All of these are issues that persons of faith consider as they determine the best decision for their lives.

One issue that sometimes divides Christian individuals and church communities is contraception. For instance, the traditional teaching of the Roman Catholic Church for centuries has been that the sexual act is for the unity of the heterosexual couple and for procreation. This was reaffirmed in a papal encyclical of 1968 that reaffirms the teaching, "Each and every marital act must of necessity retain its intrinsic relationship to the procreation of human life." Today many people and communities of faith, including United Methodists, have come to understand family planning as a choice belonging to individuals and couples as well as a necessary means of dealing with population growth and health concerns.

Birth control, as many of us know, can be one way to enhance the health of women. The Social Principles assert that those who marry are blessed by God whether or not there are children of the union.[18] The section of the Social Principles on the right to health care also advocates that women and men "have access to comprehensive reproductive health/family planning information that will serve as a means to prevent unplanned pregnancies, reduce abortions, and prevent the spread of HIV/AIDS."[19]

Any sexual ethic that we suggest must take seriously the right to health care for all persons. We may differ as to how that can be delivered and maintained, but it seems that Christ, the healer, again and again sought to restore health and well-being to men and women. United Methodist Women and other church entities have addressed the issue of reproductive health for many years.

The controversy over whether it is ever appropriate to terminate a pregnancy and who has the right to make such a decision is very much with us, as it has been for years. How might the Bible speak to us in attempting to form a sexual ethic regarding abortion? *The Oxford Guide to the Bible* states, "Abortion as such is not discussed in the Bible, so any explanation of why it is not legislated or commented on is speculative."[20] The same entry goes on to suggest that the desperate need for children would have indicated that intentional abortion would not have been approved among the Hebrew people.

It was true for many centuries that the infant mortality rate might have been as much as 50 percent and that, given diet and living conditions of the time, female fertility might have been low. Again we are reminded that the worth of a woman, a female child, and an infant girl was less than the worth of the male equivalents. In Leviticus 27, the worth of individuals in making a vow and an offering is stated with the amount to be offered according to age and sex. Basically the worth of females was a half to a third less than males.

We cannot know for sure, but it is possible that the lives of girl babies at times in ancient Israel might have been threatened. This assuredly happened in nearby cultures, and infanticide was practiced in Roman times by exposing unwanted children, mostly girls, to the elements.

Even with drastic changes in culture, better health care, and attitudes that value women as equal with men, the conflict over abortion continues. While Jesus said nothing about abortion, we seek wisdom as we form a sexual ethic that speaks to intentional termination of a pregnancy. Genesis 1:28 tells us to be fruitful and multiply, written in a time when procreation was needed to support the survival of the persecuted minority community. Our Social Principles remind us that a termination of pregnancy should not be used as a means of birth control or for gender selection.[21]

Often the current debate includes discussion of whether the fetus deserves the same rights and protections as a person. Exodus 21:22–25, which requires only payment of a fine if someone accidentally causes a miscarriage but does not injure the pregnant woman, would suggest that it does not. But other passages seem to lean the other way. Psalm 139 speaks eloquently of our being formed in our mother's womb. "My frame was not hidden from you when I was being made in secret, intricately woven in the depths of the earth" (Psalm 139:15). Luke 1:41–44 speaks of Mary's visit to Elizabeth as John leaps in his mother's womb. These last two passages witness to a view of the sacredness of life in the womb, despite our contemporary differences of opinion about when personhood begins.

The Social Principles ask us to consider the sacredness of both the woman and the unborn child. Can they really be considered separately? The General Conference of The United Methodist Church formed the present 2012 statement over many years and many sessions.[22] The debate was intense and at times volatile. No one present, as a people of faith, was casual about terminating life, anyone's life.

The reality of abortion was considered tragic, as the statement reflects. Yet it seemed necessary to some to support the legal option to a safe medical procedure. Too many stories by people from the United States were remembered of illegal "back-room" abortions causing death to both woman and child before abortion became legal here.[23] Many clinics that provide abortion services are sometimes picketed or legislated against, with critics forgetting that the same clinics offer pregnancy counseling that includes options other than terminating a pregnancy, and offer access to mammograms and birth control. Adoption is a worthy option as there are many families who desire to grow by welcoming others in. Our family includes an adopted son and adopted grandchildren. The extended family is grateful to the biological and adoptive parents who chose this option.

Pastors and counselors can recall discussing and praying with women and men caught in a situation of an unwanted pregnancy. The reasons differ from case to case. Our Social Principles speak of the "tragic conflicts of life with life."[24]

Prayer needs to be a part of any decision, as does careful attention to Scripture, tradition, reason, and experience. But even with our best efforts, we will sometimes come to conclusions that are at odds with those reached by other faithful people in the church.

RAPE AND ABUSE

We need to see the broad picture as the church. Isn't it possible that the lack of self-esteem among women and men can contribute to acts of violence that happen among us on a daily basis?

Rape has existed throughout history. It has taken centuries for society to recognize rape as a crime of violence. Read again the story of the rape of Tamar in 2 Samuel 13. This act of violent abuse was condoned, even by King David.

In Deuteronomy 22:22–29 we find laws concerning rape. The first instance is when a man rapes a virgin already engaged. If they are in the town they are both to be stoned, the woman because she did not cry out. In the second case, if the rape occurred in the country, only the man is to be killed as the woman would not have been heard if she did cry out. In the case of a virgin who is not engaged, the man shall pay fifty shekels to her father, and the rapist shall marry her and can never divorce her since he violated her. In this instance at least the violation is admitted; yet the greater crime is to the family headed by her father. We cannot forget that under these laws cited above, some women who had been raped were forced to marry and to live with their rapists. This is unthinkable for most of us today.

If we believe that rape or sexual assault is less of an issue at present, here are some statistics from the Cleveland Rape Crisis Center reporting rape statistics for 2014:

- One of every six adult American women has been the victim in an attempted or completed rape in her lifetime.
- Three percent of men, one in thirty-three, have experienced attempted or completed rape in their lifetime.
- Fifteen percent of sexual assault and rape victims are under the age of twelve.
- Seventy-three percent of sexual assaults were perpetrated by a non-stranger.[25]

These are just a few of the disturbing statistics. We continue to question the tragic reality of sexual assault. Sexual shame on the part of women and girls can be a part of this questioning. At the same time, the act of rape on the part of the man (rape is usually a male raping a female, though not always) can arise from feelings of inadequacy and defectiveness. Violence and rage are at the heart of the crime. Much too often the law has failed to protect the vulnerable. That is changing in our time. We have all heard that "no means no." This is not yet a universal understanding. There is undoubtedly more to be done to assure safety for children, women, and men.

Additionally, rape as a weapon of war is also prevalent in our time—specifically used to impart fear and shame to women as well as their family members.[26] In many cases, raped girls and women have also become trafficked as prostitutes or sexual slaves.

Human trafficking is a form of modern-day slavery in which people profit from the exploitation of others. The area of human trafficking that is often front and center in the news is sexual trafficking, specifically commercial sexual exploitation of children, although there are other forms of trafficking involving domestic workers, agricultural workers, hotel and restaurant workers, and others. Sexual trafficking is where people are profiting from the rape and sexual abuse of others, most often girls or women, although new research is coming out about the exploitation of boys. Women are made vulnerable through many channels: the media and its representation of what/how a female should look and act; sexual abuse; lack of foundational stabilities such as housing, food, clothing, and familial protection, to name a few. Sexual trafficking takes place on the street in terms of street prostitution, in massage parlors and brothels, on the Internet, and in all of our communities.

Sex traffickers use multiple tactics to lure, push, or drag women and girls into sexual exploitation, such as threats, lies, debt bondage, and physical violence. Under federal law, any minor under the age of eighteen engaged in sex work is a victim of sex trafficking regardless of whether the trafficker used force, fraud, or coercion. The average age of entry into commercial sexual exploitation (what is really just repeated sexual abuse and rape) is twelve to thirteen. Many of the youth are prepared for this type of abuse due to the sexual abuse that occurred in their younger years, knowing no other way of life.[27]

CLOSING

All of these new realities need to be considered in forming a sexual ethic for oneself as an individual and for the life of the church. I find the words of Walter Wink helpful, "Our moral task, then, is to apply Jesus' love ethic to whatever sexual mores are prevalent in a given culture. This doesn't mean everything goes. It means that everything is to be critiqued by Jesus' love commandment."[28]

Central to the Jesus we encounter in the Bible is his witness to God's desire for healthy and whole relationships, full of the promise of abundant life. As a guide to a sexual ethic that reflects Christian values, we are called to concentrate on Jesus' love and respect for all persons. This means that as we take authority to interpret Scripture, we have to concentrate on the blessing given by God in creation and on the gift of sexuality given to us to enjoy in loving relationships.

It means that we continue to let the Holy Spirit speak to us through the Scriptures as we pray, study, and seek wisdom and insight. Much of this we will do together in groups where we will share in mutual respect and know that we may continue to have differences in our interpretation of particular passages in the Bible. Understanding the Bible and human sexuality is a work in progress. Developing a sexual ethic is holy work. It is the work of God. 1 John contains a passage I often share at weddings and covenant celebrations. For me it has been the essence of Scripture for all of my life, including my sexuality:

> Beloved, let us love one another, because love is from God; everyone who loves is born of God and knows God. Whoever does not love does not know God, for God is love. God's love was revealed among us in this way: God sent his only Son into the world so that we might live through him. In this is love, not that we loved God, but that God loves us and sent his Son to be the atoning sacrifice for our sins. Beloved, since God loved us so much, we also ought to love one another. No one has ever seen God;

if we love one another, God lives in us, and God's love is perfected in us. (1 John 4:7–12)

The legacy of John Wesley and the Methodist movement understands that loving one another is active and involves working for justice for all God's people. This includes formation of a sexual ethic that offers full personhood and wholeness to everyone. We honor the ministries of the church that promote the fullness of God's design for humanity and all creation.

How does all this fit into a sexual ethic that reflects Christ's desire that everyone enjoy abundant life? We will need to pray and spend some time to discern our answer, knowing that even as we bring to the issue our faithful interpretation of what the Bible says, what our reason concludes, what our tradition implies, and what our experience tells us, we may still find ourselves differing with brothers and sisters who are equally faithful. God created us in human bodies—we are fearfully and wonderfully made. As we continue to discern and grow in our understanding of the gift of sexuality, we must remember that God has created each of us, loves us unconditionally, and desires that we love others as God in Christ loves us.

Endnotes

1. Barbara Lee, "Creating a Sexual Ethic" in *Sacred Sex*, 80.

2. Virginia Ramey Mollenkott, *Women, Men and the Bible* (New York: Crossroad Publishing), 25.

3. S. Michael Houdmann, "What does it mean that we are fearfully and wonderfully made (Psalm 139:14)?" Got Questions Ministries, accessed July 13, 2015, www.gotquestions. org/fearfully-wonderfully-made.html.

4. *The Book of Discipline of The United Methodist Church 2012*, Social Principles, 126.

5. The Campaign for a Commercial-Free Childhood, homepage, accessed December 10, 2014, www.commercialfreechildhood.org.

6. Karen R. McClintock, *Sexual Shame*, 24.

7. Ibid., 28–29.

8. *The Book of Discipline of The United Methodist Church 2012*, Social Principles, 118.

9. Bruce Birch, *To Love As We Are Loved*, 52.

10. *The Book of Discipline of The United Methodist Church 2012*, Social Principles, 109.

11. Ibid.,109.

12. Ibid., 220.

13. Eugene F. Rogers, Jr., *Sexuality and the Christian Body: Their Way into the Triune God* (New York: Blackwell Publishers, 1999), 35.

14. Walter Wink, *Homosexuality and the Bible* (Philadelphia: Fellowship Press, 1996), 2.

15. Ibid., 14.

16. Daniel A. Helminiak, What the *Bible Really Says about Homosexuality* (New Mexico: Alamo Square Press, 2007), 7.

17. Ibid., 46.

18. *The Book of Discipline of The United Methodist Church 2012*, Social Principles, 109.

19. Ibid., 127.

20. Bruce M. Metzger and Michael D. Coogan, *The Oxford Guide to the Bible,* 4.

21. *The Book of Discipline of The United Methodist Church 2012*, Social Principles, 112–114.

22. Ibid.

23. Ibid.

24. Ibid.

25. Cleveland Rape Crisis Center, homepage, accessed January 23, 2015, www. clevelandrapecrisis.org/resources/statistics.

26. "The State of the World's Children 1996," UNICEF, accessed July 7, 2015, www. unicef.org/sowc96/contents.htm?531,104.

27. Janet Orozco, director Community Based Services, David and Margaret Youth and Family Services, interview with author.

28. Walter Wink, *Homosexuality and the Bible*, 11.

✳ Bibliography

Anderson, Cheryl B. *Women, Ideology and Violence.* New York: T & T Clark, 2004.

Arias, Mortimer. *Announcing the Reign of God: Evangelization and the Subversive Memory of Jesus.* Eugene, Oregon: Wipf and Stock, 2011.

Bass, Diana Butler. *A People's History of Christianity,* New York: HarperOne, 1989.

Beach, Maxine. *The Bible: The Book that Bridges the Millennia, Part 2: Interpretation and Authority,* New York: The United Methodist Church, General Board of Global Ministries, 1999.

Berryman, Phillip. *Liberation Theology: Essential Facts About the Revolutionary Movement in Latin America and Beyond.* New York: Pantheon Books, 1987.

Birch, Bruce. *To Love As We Are Loved: The Bible and Relationships.* Nashville: Abingdon Press, 1992.

The Book of Discipline of The United Methodist Church, Nashville: United Methodist Publishing House, 2012.

Boring, M. Eugene, and Craddock, Fred B. *The People's New Testament Commentary.* Louisville: Westminster John Knox Press, 2004.

Chadwick, Henry. *The Early Church.* London: Penguin Books, 1993.

Coogan, Michael. *God and Sex: What the Bible Really Says.* New York: Twelve Hachette Book Group, 2010.

Countryman, L. William. *Dirt Greed and Sex: Sexual Ethics in the New Testament and Their Implications for Today.* Minneapolis: Fortress Press, 2007.

Eisler, Riane, *The Chalice and the Blade.* San Francisco: Harper, 1987.

Guyon, Jeanne. *Selected Writings,* (Classics of Western Spirituality series). Introduction I. Brief Biography. Mahwah, NJ: Paulist Press, 2011.

Helminiak Daniel A. *What the Bible Really Says about Homosexuality.* New Mexico: Alamo Square Press, 2007.

Kelly, J. N. D. *Early Christian Doctrines.* San Francisco: Harper, 1978.

Knust, Jennifer Wright. *Unprotected Texts: The Bible's Surprising Contradictions About Sex and Desire.* New York: HarperOne, 2011.

Lee, Barbara, "Creating a Sexual Ethic" in *Sacred Sex.* Grand Haven, MI: Splattered Ink Press, 2013.

Levine, Amy-Jill, and Brettler, Marc Zvi. *The Jewish Annotated New Testament.* New York: Oxford University Press, 2011.

MacCulloch, Diarmaid. *Christianity: The First Three Thousand Years.* London: Penguin Books, 2011.

McClintock, Karen R. Sexual Shame: *An Urgent Call to Healing.* Minneapolis: Fortress Press, 2001.

Metzger, Bruce M. *A Textual Commentary on the Greek New Testament.* New York: United Bible Societies, 1975.

Metzger, Bruce M., and Coogan, Michael D. *The Oxford Guide to the Bible.* New York: Oxford University Press, 2002.

The New Interpreter's Bible. Nashville: Abingdon Press, 1996.

The New Interpreter's Dictionary. Nashville: Abingdon Press, 2009.

Rogers, Eugene F., Jr., *Sexuality and the Christian Body: Their Way into the Triune God.* Hoboken, NJ: Wiley-Blackwell Publishers, 1999. Blackwell Publishers, 1999.

Runciman, Steven. *The Medieval Manichee.* Cambridge: Cambridge University Press, 1982.

Social Principles of The United Methodist Church 2013–2016. Nashville: The United Methodist Publishing House, 2013.

Trible, Phyllis. *God and the Rhetoric of Sexuality.* Philadelphia: Fortress Press, 1978.

Wink, Walter, *Homosexuality and the Bible,* 1996 reprint from an article that appeared in *The Christian Century,* 19.

✳ About the Author

Ellen A. Brubaker was born and raised in Muskegon, Michigan. She graduated from Muskegon High School in 1955 and attended Albion College, graduating in 1959. She taught public school for several years and did graduate work at Michigan State University and later at Eastern Michigan University, receiving an MA degree from Eastern in English language and literature. Ellen and her first husband Robert Brubaker raised four children. She entered United Theological Seminary, graduating with a Master of Divinity degree.

Ellen was ordained as an Elder in the West Michigan Conference in 1976. After serving as a pastor, she became a district superintendent in the Grand Rapids District and later served in two more appointments as a pastor. During her years under appointment, she wrote curricula for youth and adults. Her husband, Bob, died in 1987. In 1992 she married John Ross Thompson, a United Methodist clergyperson from the Western Pennsylvania Conference. John Ross became a member of the West Michigan Conference.

Following retirement as an active clergyperson, Ellen became an adjunct instructor in the Communication Studies Department at Albion College. Ellen has been actively involved in the connectional church, serving several times as a delegate to General Conference, the General Board of Finance and Administration, and for several years on the World Methodist Council Executive Committee. In her conference she has chaired the Commission on the Status and Role of Women and the Conference Board of Church and Society. The blended family of Ellen and John Ross consists of seven children with spouses and partners, sixteen grandchildren, and five great grandchildren. Ellen continues to serve as the Peace Advocate for the West Michigan Conference.

The Bible and Human Sexuality: Claiming God's Good Gift

PARTICIPANT'S GUIDE

M. GARLINDA BURTON

✳ Introduction

We are sexual beings. God made us that way. Sexuality can be celebrated and it can be exploited. It can draw us closer to the one we love or it can divide whole communities of faith. Yet, we are called to be the beloved community of healing, wholeness, reconciliation, and love. How we help one another make sense of the beauty and complexities of sexuality is the purpose of this study.

Discussing sexuality is difficult for Christians for many reasons. Many of us were raised to avoid the subject or deem it "too private." Many of us have learned no vocabulary for talking about our own sexual experiences, our understanding of sexuality, and what we do or don't believe.

However, there is good news, Ellen Brubaker writes in *The Bible and Human Sexuality,* "Human sexuality is part of who we are as human beings, created by God and called good." Sexuality, at its best, is a divine gift meant to enhance and strengthen relationships and draw us closer to our intimate partners, she explains. And there are many citations in the Bible that point to the good gift of sexuality, explicitly and implicitly, beginning with the creation stories in Genesis.

At the same time, Brubaker acknowledges that, like faith itself, our understanding and beliefs about sexuality are not informed and rooted in biblical texts alone. As she asserts, "Doctrines of the early church are a part of the story. What we were taught about sexuality, ourselves, and the church are also a part of the story. What were we taught about the relationship of men and women?"

Sexuality is personal; at the same time, how we understand sexuality has implications for us as people of faith in church and society. Issues of marriage, divorce, sexual orientation, gender identity, abortion, human trafficking, and prostitution require us to clarify our personal understanding and articulate a corporate vision of right relationships, justice, righteousness, and right relationship in the human family.

It is important that you become aware of your own beliefs, feelings, biases, and understanding when it comes to being a person of faith seeking to know God and self better. Know that you are asking questions about and wrestling with an issue that has challenged the Judeo-Christian community since the beginning. Study and exploration, prayer and reflection, are the ways of a faith-filled life. So put aside your doubts and fears and dive in; God's loving spirit is waiting to guide you.

HOW TO USE THIS GUIDE

Whether you are participating in a group study with a leader or you are going through *The Bible and Human Sexuality* on your own, taking part in this study may evoke feelings of uncertainty, fear, defensiveness, anxiety, and even conflict in your spirit. Many of us have been raised and nurtured in an environment in which sexuality is just not talked about. And many people of faith have never heard a sermon or engaged in a Sunday school discussion where sexual themes were discussed and contemporary sexual issues explored.

One way to get in touch with those feelings and use them to expand your conversation with God is to keep a journal. Journaling is a centuries-old method through which people of faith have recorded their thoughts, feelings, reflections, and questions about their faith journey. As you read and reflect on the assigned readings and biblical texts, note them in your journal. Write how you feel about what you're reading, what you remember from Sunday school lessons and sermons past, what you learned from parents and grandparents, and what statements challenge your current understanding.

If you are using this guide in a private setting, you may also want to establish a space for prayer and devotion. If possible, set a small table with a candle, cross, and even flowers and incense if you desire. The point is to create a welcoming, comfortable, and holy place where you may like to read and reflect, kneel or bow, and pray whenever the notion hits you during this study.

When using this guide for individual study and reflection, change the pronouns in the litanies, prayers, and readings to be more personal, changing them from "we are" to "I am," etc.

How each session is organized:
The study is divided into four sessions, and each lesson is organized as follows:

- *Preparation:* Assigned reading from *The Bible and Human Sexuality* by Ellen Brubaker.
- *Salient Statement:* A summary and/or direct quote from the assigned chapters for the day.
- *Centered by God's Teaching Spirit:* Suggested prayers and Scripture reading for reflection.
- *The Word and THE Word:* Concepts and questions for reflection/discussion for participants (working either in groups or alone). You should reflect on such questions as:
  - What key points were raised in the reading?
  - What was new information to me? What had I not considered before this moment?
- *Discovery:* Discover using key questions. (What were the key points raised in the reading? What was new information to me? What had I not considered before this moment?). Participants working alone may use this time to write in a journal. Participants working in a group setting may report back to the community, using the suggested questions for that session.

- *God Speaks and We Respond:* Reflect on key points and how one might respond to what she/he has discovered, individually and as part of a faith community (local, regional, national, global).
- *Closing Worship/Reflection:* A time of closing devotion, with prayers that may be used by a single participant or in a group setting. While intended to signal the end of the study time, worship may inspire an idea that you should note in your journal. Please do so.

The Word of God ... and Words about the Word

PREPARATION

Read Brubaker, Chapters 1 and 2.

SALIENT STATEMENT

"God created the process of sex, love, and birth. We may continue to discuss and discern in different ways. This is essential to growth in the faith. We need not determine right and wrong in ways that separate believers from one another" (Brubaker, Chapter 2).

CENTERED BY GOD'S TEACHING SPIRIT

Read Song of Solomon 4:1–5, followed by Matthew 5:27–30. If you are creating a worship space for yourself, you may choose to light a candle and place it on a table in your worship place.

Personal Prayer (unison)

Wondrous Creator of all good things, we come to you humbly asking for your wisdom. In your Word, we hear both a celebration of our sexual selves and warning about misuse of our sexuality.

We read stories of our forefathers, whom you adored. Some had many wives and many children by those wives. But we see in Jesus' earthly parents two people alone, joined together as partners.

Our history includes those who would name all fleshly things as bad, while the Song of Solomon clearly is a scriptural celebration of sexual delight between two people.

We want to know more from you, O God, about how we can honor our sexual selves and purify our souls, how we can stop sexual abuse and exploitation of the vulnerable, and how we can say to the church and the world that God has given us both a gift and a responsibility in creating us as sexual beings.

And so we invite you in, Great God and Light of our lives, as we work together to know you better and to follow you more faithfully. Help us to see as you would have us see. In Jesus's name. **Amen.**

REAL LIFE—REEL LIFE (optional)

The following is a personal experience that has given me perspective as I approach the topic of human sexuality in my writings and talks. Read the following story aloud:

About ten years ago, I was invited to lead a workshop for the staff at a United Methodist–related agency about sexual ethics and the church's policies on prevention of sexual misconduct and sexual harassment. I began my presentation, as I still do, by asserting that sexuality is a part of who we are as

God's creation, and that sexual behavior is natural—even good for us—in the right context.

I further said to the participants that each person had some stake in sexual behavior, if only because their birth mother had had sexual contact in order to conceive them.

At that point, one participant—a woman of about 50—got up and stormed out. She did not come back to the training, and headed straight to the human resources office to complain. Later in the day I ran into her and asked her if we could talk about what happened. She was extremely agitated and angry, but she finally told me, "My mother did NOT have sex. The way you said it was an insult to my mother."

I asked her if she could help me understand. She was furious, but she explained. "My mother did NOT have sex. She did her wifely duty and she made love with my father—her husband, by the way. It was Godly and my birth was a blessing. It was NOT sex." And with that she walked away.

That story stuck with me, and it has informed my writing and speaking on issues of sexuality, justice, and faith. For many, many of us, sexuality is difficult to discuss, particularly in the context of our faith, so much so that even talking about it gets our hackles up.

The good news, though, is that the church is beginning to talk more. We don't have all the answers. But we are willing to ask the questions. One good example is that in the last quadrennium the Connectional Table of The United Methodist Church sponsored a series of conversations among diverse members about their feelings, theological viewpoints, and cultural perspectives on the issue of homosexuality.

The members were not there to convince one another about the "rightness" or "wrongness" of one viewpoint or another; they were there to engage one another about biblical interpretation, love, and grace, and what people in their congregations and contexts were saying and struggling with. These dialogues were a humble step in a positive direction; they were confessional in nature and allowed everyone a voice and assumed everyone at the table was an ardent disciple of Jesus Christ with a hunger to do God's will and live out God's light in the world.

THE WORD AND **THE** WORD

Think about your own sexual history, experience, and what you have been taught by the church. Answer the following questions:

- What were you taught about what age was the "right" age for sexual activity?
- What did you believe as a 20-year-old about who should initiate sexual intercourse?
- How were women supposed to feel about sex?
- How were men supposed to feel about sex?
- If you ever heard a Sunday school teacher or preacher talk about sex, what were some of the things they said?
- What constitutes "good" or appropriate sexual contact? What institutes "bad" sex?
- What did your parents tell you about sexual contact, sexual behavior, or who should have sex?
- What might make one consider her/his sexual encounter "shameful"?

Note each positive answer you may give about sexuality. ("Sex was a gift." "Sex was something sacred." "I was taught that a sexual relationship was special and once-in-a-lifetime." "I learned to respect my body as a temple," etc.)

If you're working in a group, you and other participants may be asked to color with crayons or markers a piece of a puzzle cutout for each positive answer you give, and place it in the center of your group table. The goal is to make some of those positive feelings, histories, teachings, and behaviors visible so that when we're talking together at tables, we are sensitive to the fact that not every Christian person sees, feels, or considers sexuality the same way.

Review any notes you made upon reading Brubaker's Chapter 1, particularly the sections on "Song of Songs" and "Human Sexuality and the Development of Israel," and Chapter 2, particularly "The Birth Narratives" and "The Life and Ministry of Jesus—The Misfits."

1. What is the purpose of sexuality, according to the Bible?
2. Are there behaviors and norms practiced by God's people in the Old Testament that match or affirm your own views of "good" sex? What are they?
3. Are there behaviors and norms practiced by God's people in the Old Testament that run counter to your own views of "good" sexual behavior? What are they?
4. What changes, if any, do we see in the New Testament with the teachings of Jesus?
5. What information did Brubaker present that was new to you?
6. What, if any, ideas for what the church or United Methodist Women could do to better address sexuality have surfaced for you?

DISCOVERY

Review your answers and note any themes or inconsistencies—or places of discomfort. If you're working in a group, listen to the reflections of others, and make note of any information for further reflection.

NOTE: When working in a group setting, the leader may give participants time to write in their journals, or the leader may ask you or a recorder in your group to share main ideas by posting them on an "Idea Wall," which will be set up in your meeting room. Review your posts before they are shared with the larger group. You are not compelled or required to share your ideas.

GOD SPEAKS AND WE RESPOND

Review some of the key concepts in the readings, including:

- We start from different places in our understanding and comfort with the topic of sexuality, depending on our upbringing, our own histories, any trauma or abuse we've experienced, and how the subject has been engaged in our churches.
- The Bible contains both celebrations and condemnations of sexual behavior. There is also polygamy, sex outside of marriage (Abraham was not married to Hagar), rape, and sexual abuse in the Old Testament. Jesus talks about adultery and lust, briefly, but he also talks about forgiveness being more powerful than "sin," and questions why the adulterous woman was denounced and the men she "sinned with" were not (John 8:1–11).
- If we are part of God's creation and we are sexual, then our sexuality is part of who we are. We need to ask ourselves how can we celebrate it, practice it, enjoy it justly, honorably, and the way God intended.

CLOSING WORSHIP/REFLECTION
(If you are alone, read the following as a prayer)

Leader: It is by our love that we are known to be followers of Christ.

ALL: **It is by trusting that we become fully human.**

Leader: It is by changing that we hope to grow.

ALL: **What we were when we came here, we will not be when we leave, for we have met each other in the presence of God.**

Leader: Let us therefore show love for one another.

Litany by Brian Wren, 2004, Worship & Song: *Worship Resources for the 2012 General Conference*, No. 197, Abingdon Press, 2011. Adapted.

Paul, Church Patriarchy, and Fear of Flesh

PREPARATION

Read Brubaker, Chapters 3 and 4.

Make a Bible concordance or a searchable electronic version of the Bible (on your cell phone, computer, or table) available for research for this session.

SALIENT STATEMENT

"At times, Paul seems to fall back on his old interpretations. Paul was human and like all of us was a person of his culture and context. At the same time, he is able to forge ahead with new understandings as God is revealed to him. Perhaps these new insights are in part due to the leadership of the women he encountered in the development of the church" (Brubaker, Chapter 3).

CENTERED BY GOD'S TEACHING SPIRIT

Scripture Readings
"All of you who were baptized into Christ have clothed yourselves with Christ. There is neither Jew nor Greek; there is neither slave nor free; nor is there male and female, for you are all one in Christ Jesus" (Galatians 3:27–28, CEB).

"For example, wives should submit to their husbands as if to the Lord. A husband is the head of his wife like Christ is the head of the church, that is, the savior of the body" (Ephesians 5:22–23).

What I've Learned

Using two different colors of sticky notes or notecards:

- Write one thing you recall that Jesus says about sexuality. Try to pinpoint where it is written in the Bible.
- Write one thing you recall that Paul says about sexuality. Try to pinpoint where it is written in the Bible.
- Write any Scripture or idea you recall from the Bible that refers to sexuality. Try to recall the biblical book or part of the Bible where the Scripture may be recorded.

Centering Prayer (read in silence if you are studying alone)

Leader: When we pray, we are opening ourselves up to God, creating the possibility of being swept up off our feet by a great life-changing flood of grace.

ALL: **Today, O Loving God, help us to pay attention to your Word.**

Leader: Part of what we ask, Teaching God, is that you shape our prayers, and empty us to the place where we are naked, honest and thirsty. You show us our true selves.

ALL: **Today, O Nurturing God, clothe us in your love, fill us with your living water, and endow us with the power to see deeply into your heart.**

Leader: Take charge of us, O Guiding Spirit.

ALL: **Take charge, O Revealing God. We are ready to listen. Amen.**

Liturgy adapted from *The Call: Living Sacramentally, Walking Justly,* by George McClain, Tilda Norberg, and Nancy Kruh (editor). United Methodist Women, 2013, 43–45.

NOTE: If you're working in a group, the leader may show a video clip or read an article at this point. The leader will also guide you through an exercise using your sticky notes/notecards.

THE WORD AND **THE** WORD

Spend some time looking up the passages you wrote on your notecards/sticky notes. (Use a concordance, searchable electronic program, or a web search.)

If there are errors, write down the correct citations for your passages. If you've misquoted—or if you can't find a particular quotation—note that as well.

Note in your journal whether or not your answers were accurate or inaccurate, relevant or irrelevant, or just plain contradictory. Ask the recorder to jot down the group members' observations.

Now, review the following Scriptures:

- Matthew 19:1–9 (Jesus discussing marriage and divorce.)
- Hebrews 13:4 (Honoring marriage.)
- 1 Corinthians 7:3–5 (Meeting each other's sexual needs.)
- Romans 13:13–14 (Opposing "sleeping around.")
- Matthew 5:27–28 (Having lust is the same as acting on one's lust.)

Now, look up answers to the following questions in Chapter 4 of the text.

- What did early Gnostic Christians, like Pontus, say about sexuality? About women? Did they view sexuality as a gift from God? Were women viewed as equal to men in intellect or basic worth? Were women viewed as capable of making rational, mutual decisions?
- What did Augustine say about celibacy? What did Thomas Aquinas say about virtue? How does that connect with your understanding of biblical stories, people, and teachings?

- What difference does it make to have these emerging voices enter the discussion about biblical teachings, sexuality, love, and intimate relationships:
  - Women?
  - People of color?
  - People from outside the United States and Europe?
  - Young people?
  - People who are gay, lesbian, bisexual, transgender, questioning their sexuality, or those who consider themselves their allies (parents, friends, siblings, prayer partners, etc.)?
- How have some of these above teachings influenced what Christians believe, say, do, and discuss today?

DISCOVERY

Reflect on any ideas you may have attributed to the Bible that were, in fact, not in the Bible, and jot down the actual source for such information.

Review these statements from The United Methodist Church as found in *The Book of Discipline of The United Methodist Church 2012*. (Write in your journal any thoughts you have about these statements.)

1. "We affirm with Scripture the common humanity of male and female, both having equal worth in the eyes of God" (¶161E).
2. "We affirm that sexuality is God's good gift to all persons. We call everyone to be responsible stewards of this sacred gift" (¶161F).
3. "We reject social norms that assume different standards for women than for men in marriage" (¶161B).
4. "Although all person are sexual beings whether or not they are married, sexual relationships are affirmed only with the covenant of monogamous, heterosexual marriage" (¶161F).

5. "The United Methodist Church does not condone the practice of homosexuality and considers it incompatible with Christian teaching" (¶161F).
6. "Violent, disrespectful, or abusive sexual expressions do not confirm sexuality as God's good gift" (¶161H).
7. "We deplore all forms of the commercialization and exploitation of sex, with their consequent cheapening and degradation of human personality" (¶161F).

CLOSING WORSHIP/REFLECTION (unison)

God, we are just starting to understand how powerful sex is. What a gift it is. And how much we have yet to understand about how we are to use this precious gift. And we are not the first. The rape of Dinah. The love between Elkanah and his barren wife, Hannah. The lovers in Song of Songs. The redemption of Rahab. All these are stories of the sexuality of human beings.

What we need from you, O God, is help in understanding our sexual desire as one message about who we are, and to interpret that message in a way that is pleasing to you. Denial, repression, fear, and self-loathing are not your ways. But neither are abuse, exploitation, selling and buying sex, and using the Bible to shame those we may not understand. What we need, O God, is your Word written in our hearts every day and every hour. Otherwise, we will forever be tied up in knots, confused and confounded, and unsure about the gift of intimacy, union, and release that are your gift of sexuality.

Speak, Loving and Edifying God. And we'll keep listening.

Loving God, you created us for beauty, for happiness, for one another. Forgive us when we allow ugliness and abuse to obliterate the gifts of body, mind and spirit. Help us to confront abuse and injustice. In Jesus' name. **Amen.**

✳ ✳ ✳ SESSION 3

Developing a Holistic Sexual Ethic
for Today's Christians

PREPARATION

Read Brubaker, Chapter 5.

SALIENT STATEMENT

"We, as United Methodists, also believe that every person of faith who seeks to know more of Christ and God's desire for humanity should take upon herself or himself authority regarding the discernment of God's Word for God's people" (Brubaker, Chapter 5).

CENTERED BY GOD'S TEACHING SPIRIT

"You are the one who created my innermost parts; you knit me together while I was still in my mother's womb. I give thanks to you that I was marvelously set apart. Your works are wonderful—I know that very well" (Psalm 139:13–14).

Prayer (may be read as a single prayer)
Reader 1:   God calls us to health and wholeness, to present ourselves as

living sacrifices—including our sexual selves. We are to celebrate, take joy in and love our bodies and their pleasures.

Reader 2: Yet, when we are ashamed of nakedness, fearful of sexuality, unsure that sex can be good, we shame and blame others and ourselves.

ALL: **But shame doesn't help us and it doesn't honor God. What we need are new conversations, new eyes, new visions, and new appreciations.**

Reader 1: I will replace blame with prayers for and prayer with . . . *(allow participants to fill in the blank).*

Reader 2: I will replace shame with celebration of God's good creation: Me!

ALL: **I will study the Bible and dare to challenge myself and others around me to risk hearing the Word of God in new ways and from new voices.**

Reader 1: I will repent of misusing Scriptures to privilege my beliefs and my way of life at the expense of others.

Reader 2: I will invite the Holy Spirit to show me new things.

ALL: **Starting now. Starting today. Starting in this room. Starting with these friends in Christ. Amen!**

THE WORD AND **THE** WORD

Review your notes about Chapter 5 and any other notes you've made about your feelings and reflections.

Now, reflecting on all you have read and considered since the beginning of this study, consider how you might hear and understand Scripture, Brubaker's writing, your beliefs, or the statements about sexuality from The United Methodist Church if you were one of the people listed below (select two or three):

- An 11-year-old child bride of a 40-year-old man.
- The 7-year-old boy held in sexual slavery.
- The 45-year-old lesbian United Methodist Women president.
- The 32-year-old man who raped his wife.
- The wife who survived that rape.
- The married pastor having sex outside marriage.
- The woman church secretary, 40, having sex with the 35-year-old married male pastor.
- The 69-year-old widow who had a good and fulfilling marriage, but is now lonely and longing.
- The single, straight man, age 30.
- The 15-year-old boy who has been taught to abstain, but whose girlfriend, also a Christian, wants sex now.
- The girlfriend.
- Transgender woman who is new to this church.
- The gay teen, 16, who is afraid to tell his parents about his orientation.

Try to put yourselves in the shoes of the two to three people you selected and write how you feel about the church/biblical statements. How do they affirm or condemn your sexual self? How do you feel welcome or unwelcome in a church setting? Are there any people of faith you feel you can call on for support or prayer?

Brubaker asserts that all people created by God come to decisions and beliefs about their lives based, at least in part, on their generation, social location, upbringing, racial-ethnic identity, cultural identity, age, ability, and many other intersections of identities. It is easy to forget that much of what we declare to be truth may only be my truth or your truth, not THE truth or God's truth.

This exercise is an invitation to stand in someone else's shoes and to try to hear the voice of God, the teaching of Scripture, the impact of tradition, the reasoning and the experiences of those who may not be like us. God invites people of the Christian faith to embody faith, trust, respect, and coming together in Jesus Christ. This does not mean that we will always agree. The question is: Can we hear one another and learn from one another in a way that further builds up and powers up the body of Christ?

DISCOVERY

Note in your journal how the previous exercise (trying to walk in someone else's shoes) made you feel. Be specific. Did you feel afraid? Judgmental? Empowered? Reflective? Responsible? Angry? Frustrated? Pause to pray for people whose backgrounds and social locations are very different from yours, affirming them as being created in God's image and asking for God's grace and presence in their lives.

Reflect on the following statements:

- How we read and understand Scripture affects how we understand ourselves as humans, as sexual beings, and as Christians. If we lean only on those places in Paul's letters where women are told to submit and have the understanding that lust is bad and marriage is only for those who can't fight the urge to have sex, do we have sufficient information to teach us what God wants for our relationships? Why or why not?
- Also, the words of early church fathers, all faithful men, also have the misfortune of having no input from women, the sexual slaves of that day, the young men, and concubines still held by the ruling class. We have some people telling us that anything of "flesh" is bad on the one hand, and the biblical book Song of Songs celebrating fleshly delights on the other. We don't hear from same-sex partners, from

child brides, from survivors of incest—all of whom were around and part of the family of faith from the Old Testament through the Corinthian church to St. Augustine and until today.

- Our sexual ethics must consider the ones who are left out and move us from shame to faithful living and relevant theological stances. Brubaker calls for us to seize our Wesleyan quadrilateral[1] to hear the voices of the left out and oppressed, and draw upon the best of our tradition and experience. Most of all, she invites us to turn to Jesus for new insights. Jesus said many times, "You have heard it said . . . but I say." Brubaker says the question, "What would Jesus do?" is a good place to start. Jesus, God With Us, is clear about caring for children. Jesus is clear about doing no harm to other children of God. What are examples of Jesus's love, justice, kindness, forbearance, and invitation with regard to our bodies and ourselves?

CLOSING WORSHIP/REFLECTION

Reader 1: Love heals. We recover ourselves in the act and art of loving. As it is written in the Gospel of John, "Anyone who does not love is still in death."

Reader 2: Injustice kills. Shame kills. Christ came into the world not to condemn and shame us, but to give us love and life in abundance. That includes a life of healthy, good sex—a life free of exploitation, violence, pornography, and lust for overpowering the vulnerable.

Reader 1: We, the Church of Jesus Christ, declare a sexual ethic of obedience, justice, health, affirmation, and love. We declare an ethic that is a wide doorway that receives all whom need human love and fellowship.

Reader 2: But it is narrow enough to keep hatred, envy, pride, shame, and loathing out. The doors of our church will be a gateway to your eternal kingdom, O God.

Reader 1: Jesus taught us, and our denomination has declared, that all people are of sacred worth. As we continue to talk about and struggle with sexuality, we are sure of this: that every person created by God is of sacred worth. And there is a place at the welcome table for each one.

Endnote

1. To learn more, read "Our Theological Task" from *The Book of Discipline of The United Methodist Church 2012*, 78–89.

Session 4

Countering Shame and Blame with Love and Ethical Action

PREPARATION

Read Brubaker, Chapter 6.

SALIENT STATEMENT

"We need to develop a sexual ethic for our time that covers individual and family sexuality, but goes on to address the desperate need for sexual justice for innocent persons who are victimized day after day. Some of these victims live closer to us than we want to believe" (Brubaker, Chapter 6).

CENTERED BY GOD'S TEACHING SPIRIT

"Jesus turned to the woman and said to Simon, 'Do you see this woman? When I entered your home, you didn't give me water for my feet, but she wet my feet with tears and wiped them with her hair. You didn't greet me with a kiss, but she hasn't stopped kissing my feet since I came in. . . . This is why I tell you that her many sins have been forgiven; so she has shown great love. The one who is forgiven little loves little.' Then Jesus said to her, 'Your sins are forgiven'" (Luke 7:44–45; 47–48, CEB).

Prayer

Read the following as a prayer if you're studying alone:

Reader 1: The people walking in darkness have seen a great light.

Reader 2: On those living in a pitch-dark land, light has dawned.

Reader 3: The Lord is my light and my salvation; whom shall I fear?

Reader 4: Jesus said to them, "I am the light of the world."

Reader 5: Then shall your light break forth like the dawn, and your healing shall spring up speedily; your righteousness shall go before you; the glory of God shall be your rear guard.

(Pause for three seconds.)

Reader 6: God With Us, Emmanuel, your Word gives light, and imparts understanding to the simple.

Reader 7: Your Word is a lamp to my feet and a light to my path.

Reader 8: I will turn the darkness before them into light, the rough places into level ground.

Reader 9: In Christ is the light of humanity.

Reader 1: Bear witness to the light. In all you are. In all you do. In the healthy, loving sexuality you share. When you shine the light on the sexual sickness and exploitation and injustice that we battle as God's people, we bear witness to the light.[1]

THE WORD AND **THE** WORD

Brubaker reminds us that shame has historically colored or even stymied our ability to have open conversations about our sexual selves and our bodies. We are descendants of people who covered up naked statues and even required furniture legs to be covered during the Victorian Era, because we have made "shame" and "shaming" central to our sexual ethics. She quotes the Rev. Karen A. McClintock as saying, "A pervasive sense of shame is the ongoing premise that one is fundamentally bad, inadequate, defective, unworthy, or not fully valid as a human being" (Brubaker, Chapter 6).

Reflect on these statements from *The Book of Resolutions:*

- "We encourage women in counsel with husbands, doctors, and pastors to make their own responsible decisions concerning the personal and moral questions surrounding the issue of abortion."[2]
- "Therefore, be it resolved, that The United Methodist Church dedicate itself to a ministry of Christ-like hospitality and compassion to persons of all sexual orientations."[3]
- "Any sexually explicit material that depicts children is pornographic."[4]
- "The vast majority of pornography is inextricably linked to oppression of women. . . . Female bodies are treated as objects and commodities . . ."[5]
- "It is estimated that more than 130 million girls and women alive today have undergone female genital mutilation/cutting, primarily in Africa and, to a lesser extent, in some countries in the Middle East."[6] NOTE: Female genital mutilation is most often used to insure the chastity of brides and to remove the clitoris to prevent her from enjoying sexual pleasure, thus becoming loose or wanton.
- "Rape during wartime constitutes many individual and group acts of violence perpetrated by soldiers against girls and women of the enemy countries, or opposing sides, often under orders. Thus, rape, in effect, is used as an extension of warfare."[7]

As you read the denomination's statements, write in your journal or on note-cards, your answers to these questions:

1. Where in our church's pronouncements can we find messages that sex can be enjoyed and celebrated?
2. What, then, do our church's sexual ethics tell us about power, consent, and shame? What do your personal ethics—not just what you believe, but how you live—tell you about those things?
3. What do we need more of in the church with regard to sexuality?

DISCOVERY

Now, reflect on what you have discovered about yourself during this study in regard to your own sexuality, beliefs about sexuality, or general sexual ethics. Write in your journal or offer your thoughts in the form of a prayer. Consider these additional questions:

- What has the church agreed upon regarding when sex is misused?
- Where are we growing as a church?
- What information was new to you today that will keep you thinking for a while?

GOD SPEAKS AND WE RESPOND

Review some of the key concepts from the assigned readings:

- Shame has no place in a healthy sexual relationship, and the church needs to stop using shame as a weapon or backup when we get to a place of disagreement about human sexuality.

- When sex hurts, wounds, humiliates, dehumanizes, and exploits, however, the church should and has spoken forcefully and clearly. Maybe not clearly enough for some, and we could add more money and action at all levels to address human trafficking, sexual violence, etc.—but there are places of agreement within the church. And one of those areas of agreement is that sexual slavery, exploitation, and violence are wrong.

- Change is always occurring and change within the church is no exception. Marriage has moved from being a business transaction to get a man free sex and sons and another man cattle and land, to what it is considered today—at its best—a sacred connection. And this change happened within the church. Our sexual ethics have changed and are changing and will continue to change. The key is to stay focused on what Jesus, God's love, and God's grace in the flesh, would have us do and be in this moment.

- There are people we are not hearing from when we talk about the spectrum of sexual issues. United Methodist Women members have been exceptional in hearing from and working with organizations around the world that are addressing human trafficking, reproductive health, and stopping rape as a weapon. But there are others whose stories we refuse to hear, people we fear, people we loathe because we don't want them to challenge our biases. Part of creating a sexual ethic for ourselves and for our church is asking who should be at the table and which voices should be valued. Then, we need to listen.

Write in your journal one positive concept you've learned about sexuality during this study. Offer a prayer of thanksgiving for that learning.

Write down at least one action you will take because of what you've learned in this study. (Examples: Join other church women's groups working on behalf of survivors of sexual abuse or human trafficking; sponsoring a workshop on sexual and domestic violence in your church or community; developing a small-group class on healthy sexuality). Include a timeline and action steps, plus the names of two people you will invite to work with you.

CLOSING WORSHIP/REFLECTION

Sing or recite the chorus of "Balm in Gilead," No. 375, in The United Methodist Hymnal.

There is a balm in Gilead
to make the wounded whole;
There is a balm in Gilead
to heal the sin-sick soul

Litany (May also be said as a prayer)

Leader: Discussing sexuality is difficult for us, O God.

ALL: **We know we don't have all the answers, but we keep trying.**

Leader: We want to do the right thing. We want to be open. We want to be holy. Help us, O God.

ALL: **From the cowardice that does not face new truths, from the laziness that is content with half-truths,**

Leader: From the arrogance that thinks it knows all the truth,

ALL: Deliver us today, good Lord.

*Last four lines of litany adapted from a prayer "From the Church in Kenya" Wild Goose Resource Group, admin. by GIA Publications, Inc., (copyright 1999), No. 179, *Word & Song: Worship Resources for the 2012 General Conference.* Abingdon Press, 2011.

(*Pause for 10 seconds.*)

Reader 1: We've struggled with a lot. We've laughed. We've disagreed. We've challenged. We've been challenged. And yet we are still the church, together and separately. We better understand and can celebrate the gift of sexuality, which we received at our creation.

Reader 2: As beings made in the holy image of God, we celebrate bodies built for work and pleasure, voices made for worship and praise, and ears made to hear all that God in Christ would teach us.

ALL: **God is still breathing life into human beings and declaring us good! Good! And so, as sisters and brothers sanctified in Christ, we will go forth from this place, and work for wholeness, peace, justice, right relationships, and reconciliation, so that all people may discover their goodness.**

Leader: In the name and for the sake of Jesus the Christ, who brings healing and hope to us all. **Amen.**

Endnotes

1. Prayer inspired by Isaiah 9:2, Psalm 27:1, John 8:12, Isaiah 58:8, Psalm 119:105, Isaiah 42:16.

2. *The Book of Resolutions of The United Methodist Church 2012,* (Nashville: United Methodist Publishing House, 2012), 120.

3. Ibid., 130.

4. Ibid., 156.

5. Ibid., 157.

6. Ibid., 248.

7. Ibid., 248.

Resources on Sexuality and the Church

Anderson, Cheryl. *Ancient Laws and Contemporary Controversies: The Need for Inclusive Biblical Interpretation*. New York: Oxford University Press, 2009.

Anderson, Cheryl B. *Women, Ideology and Violence*. New ed. London: Bloomsbury T&T Clark, 2006.

Boring, M. Eugene and Fred B. Craddock. *The People's New Testament Commentary*. Louisville, KY: Westminster John Knox Press, 2010.

Brotherson, Laura. *And They Were Not Ashamed: Strengthening Marriage Through Sexual Fulfillment*. Inspire Books, 2004.

Cheung, Patrick. *Radical Love: Introduction to Queer Theology*. New York: Seabury Books, 2011.

Coakley, Sarah. *God, Sexuality and Self: An Essay on the Trinity*. New York: Cambridge University Press, 2013.

Coleman, Monica A. *The Dinah Project: A Handbook for Congregational Response to Sexual Violence*. Cleveland: The Pilgrim Press, 2004.

De la Torre, Miguel. *Out of the Shadows, Into the Light: Christianity and Homosexuality*. Atlanta: Chalice Press, 2009.

Dines, Gail. *Pornland: How Porn Has Hijacked Our Sexuality*. Boston: Beacon Press, 2010.

Fortune, Marie M. *Is Nothing Sacred? The Story of a Pastor, the Women He Sexually Abused, and the Congregation He Nearly Destroyed.* United Church Press, 1999.

Gaede, Beth Ann, editor. *When a Congregation Is Betrayed: Responding to Clergy Misconduct.* Herndon, VA: The Alban Institute, 2006.

Falls, Abraham. *Human Trafficking: A Global Perspective of Modern Day Human Trafficking and Sex Slavery.* Kindle ebook, 2014.

Hepburn, Stephanie and Rita J. Simon. *Human Trafficking Around the World: Hidden in Plain Sight.* New York: Columbia University Press, 2013.

Jensen, Robert. *Getting Off: Pornography and the End of Masculinity.* Brooklyn, NY: South End Press, 2007.

Jung, Patricia Beattie and Darryl W. Stephens, editors. *Professional Sexual Ethics: A Holistic Ministry Approach.* Minneapolis: Fortress Press, 2013.

Lee, Barbara. *Sacred Sex: Replacing the Marriage Ethic with a Sexual Ethic.* Second Edition. Grand Haven, MI: Splattered Ink Press, 2015.

Martin, Dale B. *Sex and the Single Savior: Gender and Sexuality in Biblical Interpretation.* Louisville, KY: Westminster John Knox Press, 2006.

McClain, George, Tilda Norberg and Nancy Krub, editor. *The Call: Living Sacramentally, Walking Justly.* New York: United Methodist Women, 2013.

McClintock, Karen A. *Sexual Shame: An Urgent Call for Healing.* Minneapolis: Augsburg Fortress Press, 2001.

Merrick, James R. A., Stephen M. Garrett, R. Albert Mohler Jr., Peter E. Enns, Michael F. Bird, Kevin J. Vanhoozer, John R. *Five Views on Biblical Inerrancy.* Grand Rapids, MI: Zondervan Press, 2013.

Parker, Evelyn L., editor. *The Sacred Selves of Adolescent Girls: Hard Stories of Race, Class, and Gender.* Cleveland: The Pilgrim Press, 2006.

The Book of Discipline of The United Methodist Church 2012. Nashville: The United Methodist Publishing House, 2012.

Thistlewaite, Susan Brooks. *Women's Bodies as Battlefield: Christian Theology and the Global War on Women.* New York, NY: Palgrave Macmillan, 2015.

Wangila, Mary Nyangweso. *Female Circumcision: The Interplay of Religion, Culture and Gender in Kenya.* (From the *Women from the Margins* series). Maryknoll, NY: Orbis Books, 2007.

Weems, Renita J. *What Matters Most: Ten Lessons in Living Passionately from the Song of Solomon.* West Bloomfield, MI: Walk Worthy Press, 2004.

West, Traci C. *Disrupting Christian Ethics: When Racism and Women's Lives Matter.* Louisville, KY: Westminster John Knox Press, 2006.

Williams, Demetrius K. *An End to This Strife: The Politics of Gender in African American Churches.* Minneapolis: Fortress Press, 2004.

United Methodist Women Resources

On Maternal Health:
www.unitedmethodistwomen.org/maternal-child-health

On Reproductive Health as a Global Issue:
www.unitedmethodistwomen.org/news/stumbling-over-reproductive-health

On Human Trafficking:
www.unitedmethodistwomen.org/human-trafficking

On Domestic Violence:
www.unitedmethodistwomen.org/domestic-violence

On Contraception:
www.unitedmethodistwomen.org/news/
first-time-anyone-talked-to-me-about-contraception

✸ About the Author

M. Garlinda Burton, a United Methodist deaconess living and working in Nashville, Tennessee, is a writer, editor, and director of the Nashville Freedom School Partnership, a summer literacy and cultural enrichment program for low-income children of color. She has her own consulting ministry called *MotherWit*.

Consecrated a deaconess in 2014, Burton is a frequent contributor to print and audiovisual resources on justice for women, people of color, children, and the poor. She retired in 2012 after 33 years working for United Methodist Church agencies, most recently as general secretary of the General Commission on the Status and Role of Women. Shortly after, she began work with Freedom Schools, a program created by the Children's Defense Fund in Washington, D.C.

A popular speaker and retreat leader, Burton enjoys cooking, reading novels, road trips, graphic design, traveling with her mother, and learning from young people, particularly her grandchildren.

Other Resources from United Methodist Women

The Bible and Human Sexuality: Claiming God's Gift in Spanish
Ellen A. Brubaker
ISBN: 978-1-940182-35-3
M3274
$10

The Bible and Human Sexuality: Claiming God's Gift in Korean
Ellen A. Brubaker
ISBN: 978-1-940182- 36-0
M3273
$10

The Bible and Human Sexuality: Claiming God's Gift, Kindle version
in English
Ellen A. Brubaker
ISBN: 978-1-940182-37-7
$5.35

response magazine, May 2016 issue focusing on the Bible and
human sexuality

Place your order with:
United Methodist Women Mission Resources
1-800-305-9857

The Bible and Human Sexuality web page:
www.unitedmethodistwomen.org/sexuality-bible